THE CONSERVER SOCIETY

THE CONSERVER SOCIETY

Karl E. Henion II
University of Texas at Austin

Thomas C. Kinnear
University of Michigan

Proceedings Series

AMERICAN MARKETING ASSOCIATION

222 S. Riverside Plaza-Chicago, Illinois 60606-(312) 648-0536

©American Marketing Association
1979

Printed in the U.S.A.

Cover Design by Mary Jo Krysinski
utilizing the basic International
Graphic Symbols for Ecology

Library of Congress Cataloging in Publication Data

Main entry under title:

The Conserver society.

  Proceedings of a conference held Nov. 11, 1979 at the University of Texas.
  1. Environmental policy--Congresses. 2. Human ecology--Congresses. 3. Marketing--Congresses.
I. Henion, Karl E. II. Kinnear, Thomas C. III. American Marketing Association.
HC79.E5C6173   301.31   79-17463
ISBN 0-87757-127-9

TABLE OF CONTENTS

	Page
Foreword	ix
Preface	xi

I. THE CONSERVER SOCIETY — 1

1. Imperatives of the Conserver Society *Garrett Hardin* — 3

2. Scarcity as an Intellectual Resource *Douglas M. Costle* — 16

3. Canada's Conserver Society Studies: Their Nature and Impact *Stanley J. Shapiro* — 23

II. THE CONSERVER — 41

4. The Conserver Society? Consumers' Attitudes and Behaviors Regarding Energy Conservation *Jeffrey S. Milstein* — 43

5. Construction and Validation of a Scale to Measure Socially Responsible Consumption Behavior *John H. Antil and Peter D. Bennett* — 51

6. Identifying the Socially and Ecologically Concerned Segment Through Life-Style Research: Initial Findings *Michael A. Belch* — 69

7. An Attitudinal and a Behavioral Index of Energy Conservation *Patrick E. Murphy, Gene R. Laczniak and Richard K. Robinson* — 82

8. Consumer Energy Patterns in Canada: Indicators for the Conserver Society *J. R. Brent Ritchie, John D. Claxton and Gordon H. G. McDougall* — 92

		Page
	9. Consumer Energy Conservation Research Activity in Canada *L. G. McCabe and Carman W. Cullen*	110
	10. Government and the Energy Conscious Consumer: The Appliance Energy Labeling Program *Kenneth L. Bernhardt*	120
III.	CONSERVATION TODAY	133
	11. A Sensible Approach to Resource Conservation *Lloyd Bentsen*	135
	12. Historical Sketch of Resource Recovery and Status of Energy Retrieval from Waste *Ronald E. Schwegler*	141
	13. Recycling at Reynolds Metals *David P. Reynolds*	149
	14. Recycling: Yesterday's Image Builder is Today's Insurance Policy *F. Lewis Shirley*	154
	15. The Department of Energy Program for the Recovery of Energy and Materials from Urban Waste *Donald K. Walter*	163
	16. Causes, Controls, and Confusions *W. J. Coppoc*	175
	17. Save a Tree Bags: The Marketing of an Ecological Product *Kim Marienthal*	186
IV.	THE CONSERVER SOCIETY: HOW DO WE GET THERE?	191
	18. A Marketing Approach to Energy Conservation *Arthur Sterngold and Philip Kotler*	193

FOREWORD

The Conserver Society is a quadrennial follow-up to the first Ecological Marketing Workshop held in 1975. That one initiated the present series of educational workshops sponsored by the Marketing Education Division of the American Marketing Association.

These small workshops, whose participants are made up principally of the authors, session chairmen and discussants themselves, are planned to identify and discuss basic issues in specialized areas of marketing. Their educational purpose is to enrich the discipline and, hopefully, the society at large.

On behalf of the Marketing Education Division, I would like to express appreciation to Professors Karl E. Henion II of the University of Texas at Austin and Thomas C. Kinnear of the University of Michigan for their leadership roles in designing and developing these pioneering workshops in marketing. Their successful efforts have set a high standard, which is being met, for other workshops activities of the Marketing Education Division.

The topics, papers, speeches, and participants represented in this volume and at the conference, as well as the interactive nature of the conference discussions, represent a satisfying accomplishment of the goals established for the Marketing Education Division.

Eugene J. Kelley
Vice President 1979-1980
Marketing Education Division

PREFACE

In the early 1970's marketing researchers began to conduct empirical studies in the content area known as ecological marketing. Buttressed by a growing body of literature, the area had stimulated enough interest by mid-decade to justify holding a national conference devoted to the subject. In 1975 such a conference was held under the sponsorship of the American Marketing Association and it resulted in the publication of 15 papers. The dominant theme of the conference was a call for promoting the societal causes of improved environmental quality and resource conservation by means of more enterprise in the private sector and less regulation in the public sector.

From 1975 to 1979 social marketing writers contributing to this new field -- one that conceptually overlaps both micromarketing and macromarketing -- concentrated principally on energy conservation issues. As the decade drew to a close, a national reaction against government regulation in the energy and environmental spheres began to take hold, making the theme of the 1975 conference still more relevant.

Consequently, the same theme recurred in 1979 at a second AMA conference devoted to ecological marketing. Many felt that the current anti-regulatory mood in the United States called for government and business to strike a better balance (in the past more in the former's favor) in the division of responsibility for the management of negative social externalities. However, at the 1979 conference this basic theme competed with different, sometimes antithetical, themes with the result that ecological marketing was seen to be approaching a kind of intellectual crossroads. Overall, the Conference provided a forum for the exchange and stimulation of thought and fact dealing with opportunities to be found in a Conserver Society by elements of a free enterprise system.

Called "The Conserver Society" -- a name inspired by, and eagerly borrowed from, our Canadian friends -- the 1979 conference was held at The University of Texas at Austin from November 11 to 13. The 18 papers presented make up the contents of this book.

These papers represent the views of diverse and challenging minds with varied and rich backgrounds in business, government and academe. Authors from the business sector include: the chief executive officer of one of the world's largest aluminum companies; the president and owner of a small ecology-related company; a former vice president of a major oil company; a resource recovery manager from the world's largest company in the waste collection and disposal field; and an executive of a leading beverage company.

Authors from the government sector include: a U.S. Senator who chairs the Joint Economic Committee of the U.S. Congress; an administrator who heads the U.S. Environmental Protection Agency; leading energy conservation experts from the Canadian Government and from the Department of Energy and the Federal Trade Commission of the United States Government.

Academic authors include several Canadians who have made outstanding contributions to the widely respected series of conserver society studies in Canada; also a group of American professors of marketing, including one of its premier conceptualizers and intellectual trailblazers; and finally a scientist whose influence in intellectual circles extends far beyond his fields of biology, genetics and evolution to the policy areas of pollution and population control.

These authors have made valuable contributions to the enrichment and diffusion of knowledge dealing with "The Conserver Society" and we are in their debt. We also thank our session chairpersons: George Fisk, Director of the Management Research Center at Syracuse University; Sidney R. Galler, Deputy Assistant Secretary of Commerce for Environmental Affairs; James R. Taylor, holder of the Sebastian S. Kresge Chair in Marketing, University of Michigan; and Professor Phillip D. White of the University of Colorado. And we thank our discussion leaders -- Don L. Fitch, Vice President, Browning Ferris Industries; Professor Thomas A. Klein, University of Toledo; Professor Steven E. Permut, School of Organization and Management, Yale University; and William I. Rothbard, Federal Trade Commission. These session chairpersons and discussion leaders made invaluable contributions by stimulating and helpfully guiding the free exchange of views at the Conference, thereby insuring its success.

We acknowledge the encouragement and help we received, during the planning of the Conference, from Keith K. Cox, AMA President (1979-80) and Eugene Kelley, AMA Vice President, Marketing Education Division; and, during the publication phase, from Editor Donald L. Shawver and Publication Manager Joan Perell of AMA Professional Publications.

We wish to thank several college deans for generous financial assistance. They are Gilbert R. Whitaker, Jr., Graduate School of Business, University of Michigan; and from the University of Texas at Austin: Robert D. King, College of Liberal

Arts; George Kozmetsky, Graduate School of Business; and A. R. Schrank, College of Natural Sciences. A great debt is also owed Robert E. Witt, Chairman of the Department of Marketing Administration at the University of Texas at Austin for the countless ways -- financial and otherwise -- in which he has supported this undertaking.

Behind every editor and conference chairman stands a team of devoted staff that makes a book and conference go. A word of thanks is therefore owed the following students from the University of Texas at Austin: Russell Gregory, Kimberly McKean, Marilyn Worley, Mattie Brewer, Diana King, Kenneth D. Strickland, Jeffrey S. Tunis, and, especially, George Haley, who flawlessly coordinated and managed most of the technical operations and many of the editing tasks necessary to get the book ready for publication.

Karl E. Henion II
Thomas C. Kinnear

PART ONE

THE CONSERVER SOCIETY

This part of the book defines the Conserver Society, explaining the concepts, philosophies and problems entailed in its creation and nurturing.

IMPERATIVES OF THE CONSERVER SOCIETY

Garrett Hardin
University of California, Santa Barbara

Those who live in the midst of an ongoing revolution seldom know what the revolution is all about; that insight is left for later generations. Nevertheless, participants cannot help but speculate on the meaning of the events they take part in; to a certain extent their speculations help create the meaning.

That we are on the way to becoming a conserver society is agreed to by almost everyone now (reluctantly by some). Labeling the predecessor society now drawing to a close is not so easy. I think it would be wrong to call it a non-conserving society, or a wasting society, because non-conservation and wastage were not conscious or even desired aims of the expiring order. Drawing on a coinage of the 1960's I prefer to call that world the "Go-Go" society. This title emphasizes the endearing mindlessness of the "Soaring Sixties," as a press-agent called that decade. Like happy idiots we just plunged ahead at full speed, mindless of the consequences of our actions. Some of the major distinctions between the two societies are laid out in Table 1, which will serve as an outline for my argument. The following discussion is tied to this table by key numbers in parentheses.

The basic assumption (1) of a Go-Go society is that the universe of action is limitless; conservers assume a limited universe. From these differing assumptions there naturally follow different recommendations for action. In the Go-Go society (2) consumption is regarded as a basic good, whereas conservers prefer to conserve. Esthetics (3) follows from assumptions and actions: the inhabitants of Go-Go seek and obtain their joy from rapid turnover, while conservers look for ways of prolonging joy by restricted consumption.

Historical ages overlap: no more striking example of this can be found than a marvelous coincidence of events that occurred on the 22nd of April, 1970 (Brooks 1973). On that day, Henry Ross Perot of Dallas, Texas suffered a paper loss in the stock market of $450,000,000. This was only a third of his total theoretical worth, but it was more money in real terms than J. Pierpont Morgan possessed at the time of his death in 1913. While Perot was losing this fantastic sum of money on Wall Street, the rest of the nation was celebrating the first "Earth Day." This carefully manufactured event was aimed at making people conscious of the limitedness of our world and of

TABLE 1. SOME THINGS THAT ARE CHANGING

Characteristic	The "Go-Go" Society
1. Universe assumed	Limitless
2. Basic good	Consumption
3. Esthetic ideal	Rapid turnover a joy
4. Predominant fashion	"Conspicuous consumption" (Veblen)
5. Energy saving	A dubious good
6. Labor saving	An unquestioned good
7. Travel, mobility	A public good
8. Role of cryptic commons	"Externalities" lead to "progress"
9. Damage: burden of proof	"Innocent until proven guilty"
10. Analysis of problems	Segmental, narrow
11. Enterprisers	Very active
12. Product evolution	Fast
13. Wastefulness	Great
14. Predominant attitude:	
a. Viewed from "Go-Go"	Adventurous
b. Viewed by Conserver	Frantic
15. Control of system	By market forces
16. Errors corrected	Through economic loss, failures
17. Type of society	Contract society (Maine)
18. Objective freedom	Greater
19. Psychological freedom	Less (?)
20. Value of advertising	
a. Informational	A public good
b. Competitive	A public good, in part

TABLE 1. SOME THINGS THAT ARE CHANGING

Characteristic	The Conserver Society
1. Universe assumed	Limited
2. Basic good	Conservation
3. Esthetic ideal	Lingering enjoyment sought
4. Predominant fashion	Conspicuous penury
5. Energy saving	An undoubted good
6. Labor saving	Dubious good; with unemployment, a bad
7. Travel, mobility	A public bad
8. Role of cryptic commons	To be unmasked, eliminated
9. Damage: burden of proof	"Guilty until proven innocent"
10. Analysis of problems	Ecological; broad, at times murky
11. Enterprisers	Relatively inactive
12. Product evolution	Slow
13. Wastefulness	?
14. Predominant attitude:	
a. Viewed from "Go-Go"	Stodgy
b. Viewed by Conserver	Tranquil
15. Control of system	By bureaucracies
16. Errors corrected	Through detection of malfeasance
17. Type of society	Status society
18. Objective freedom	Less
19. Psychological freedom	Potentially greater
20. Value of advertising	
a. Informational	A public good
b. Competitive	A public bad

the necessity for conservation, which indeed it did rather well. The paper wealth and paper losses of the Texas billionaire were highly theoretical, but in a symbolic way his activity epitomized the old world that was passing away, a world in which rapid turnover of all goods--material and theoretical-- is regarded as a good and enjoyable thing in itself, whereas the promoters of the new world strive for a minimization of turnover and a maximization of lingering enjoyment.

Thorstein Veblen (1899), denying the sufficiency of the model of the "economic man" in the explanation of human action, pointed to the powerful motivation of "conspicuous consumption" in what we now call the Go-Go world (4). The conserving society follows a contrasting fashion which might be called "conspicuous penury." We see the evidence in the patched and tattered clothes of Hippies, Beatniks, commune dwellers and (paradoxically) among some of the wealthy youth of "high society." The poor little rich girl who is too deprived by her environment to be able naturally to achieve conspicuous penury can buy it "off the shelf" (for a high price) in the form of pre-faded, pre-patched jeans.

Our revolution involves an about-face in attitude towards energy and labor. In the old world, energy saving (5) was regarded as hardly worthwhile; in those dear dead days our euphoria over the prospects of peaceful atomic energy led us to believe that fusion energy, when achieved, would make electricity so cheap that it would not pay to meter it. *Sancta simplicitas*! It is now hard to believe that we took this possibility seriously so recently as a mere ten years ago. Now, even the vested interests of the electrical and gas utilities are urging us to reduce the use of their products. Who, ten years ago, would have thought that these profit-maximizing enterprises would ever seek to minimize consumption, and turnover?

Labor saving (6) is the other side of the coin. Formerly one had only to label an invention "labor saving" to have it immediately approved of. Now we have our doubts--doubts raised in the sharpest form when we contemplate the poor countries of the world (the so-called "Third World"). Poor countries almost without exception have an unemployment rate that runs to 30 percent or more. How can it possibly benefit such countries to save on labor and create more unemployment? The answer to this question is so obvious that it took us a mere twenty years to see it, something of a speed record in public perception. More than anybody else, E. F. Schumacher (1973) brought us to this realization with his great phrase, "appropriate technology." For a capital-poor country suffering from high unemployment the appropriate technology is labor-intensive, not capital-intensive. This is an undoubted truth, but we were blind to it during the early decades of so-called "foreign aid." Our own enterprisers had machinery they wanted to sell through the bureaucracy that controls foreign aid, but they had no labor to sell (which was not needed by the poor countries anyway). It was not to the interests of our enterprisers to raise the question of appropriate technology.

Sauce for the goose is sauce for the gander. If it is not a good thing to introduce labor-saving technology into a country with 30 percent unemployment, neither is labor saving a good thing in a country with 6 percent unemployment. For decades now our official unemployment rate has not been significantly below that figure, and everyone knows that much "hidden unemployment" goes uncounted. We used to think that inflation and unemployment were trade-offs--the more of one, the less of the other. Now we know that we can have both, and there is nothing on the horizon to suggest that we will ever solve the unemployment problem in a Go-Go world that encourages the waste of resources and capital while conserving labor. Perhaps by the year 2000 we will recognize that the truth that applies to poor countries applies also to the rich.

The ramifications of the coming reversal in attitude are multitudinous; I will mention only one (7). All travel requires an expenditure of energy. If the conservation of energy is good, a heavy burden of proof falls on the person who says that travel is a good thing. The Go-Go society mindlessly assumes that it is; a conserver society assumes that it is not-- that is, that travel is not *per se*, a good, though the "side effects" of moving from one place to another may be good. The **pos**tulated good of the side effects must be balanced against the intrinsic bad of energy use. When we fully accept this change in orientation, the whole tourist industry will come under serious attack. Millions of people benefit in a particular and individualistic way from tourism, but for society as a whole the net benefits of travel are undoubtedly now negative. Travel continues to be promoted, without challenge, in a world of increasing fuel shortages because most policy is determined by the few people who make a large profit rather than by the many who suffer small per capita losses even though these losses, in the aggregate, exceed the aggregate of personal profits. This is the way any politico-economic system naturally works, in the absence of contrived restraints.

The tourist industry can be used to illustrate another principle with which we seldom come to grips. This is the "too much of a good thing" principle (Sparrow 1977). The problem is most sharply illustrated in the paradox of bringing the wilderness to the people. In Howard Zahniser's classic definition, "A Wilderness, in contrast to those areas where man and his own works dominate the landscape, is . . . an area where the earth and its community of life are untrammelled by man, where man himself is a visitor who does not remain" (Hardin 1969). Whatever the values of wilderness--esthetic, spiritual, or physiological--they can be enjoyed only if people are transported to the edge of a wilderness so that they can enter it. This transportation we might say is a good thing. But if we build a four-lane highway into the center of a wilderness, the good we call "wilderness" utterly disappears. There can, in a word, be too much of a good thing, in this case transportation. The same principle applies, though not quite so sharply, to tourism in general. To visit people of a markedly different culture is indeed a good thing, since this activity diminishes our ethnocentrism, enlarges our sympathies, and in general deepens insight into our own culture. But the value of this good thing disappears as the number of tourists increases. In large numbers, tourists become channelized in their peregrinations through other lands, losing most of the meaningful contacts with other cultures. Ultimately, visitors may overwhelm and destroy the culture they visit. Tourism, pursued on a large scale, destroys the values it seeks. "Fly to this unspoiled, exotic land!" says the travel poster, thereby doing its best to destroy the beauty it praises.

In the creation of laws and regulations it is easy to say *yes* or *no*, but very difficult to say *enough, but not too much*. Yet the preservation of much of the variety and beauty of this world depends on recognizing the too-much-of-a-good-thing principle and devising laws that take account of it. As far as tourism is concerned the present escalation of the energy shortage is a good thing. If petroleum some day sells for a thousand dollars per barrel the variety and beauty of the world will be protected and greatly enhanced, even though only a few people will then be able to enjoy these good things. But few is better than none--and none is the end result of utterly cheap energy.

DOING AWAY WITH THE "TRAGEDY OF THE COMMONS"

Many of the contrasts (8) between the new world and the old are connected with the "tragedy of the commons" (Hardin 1968; developed at length in Hardin 1972). In the individualistically organized Go-Go society enterprisers are permitted to throw the waste products of their manufacturing facilities into the common property of the atmosphere and the stream, thereby achieving higher "efficiency." The harm thus done to society is attributed to the "externalities" of industry--meaning that the negative gains are external to the ledger books of the enterprisers. It is a central tenet of "welfare economics," as developed by Pigou (1920), that social waste can be minimized only if such externalities are internalized. When they are not, when externalities can be freely imposed on the unmanaged commons, the resulting politico-economic system can be labeled "commonism" (Hardin 1977). A commons that is managed by bureaucrats is what we call "socialism." When an unmanaged commons is converted to private property, managed by individual owners, "privatism" is the result.

The tragedy of the commons arises from the fact that if, among a number of individuals enjoying the freedom of a commons, one person should elect *not* to over-exploit it he will not be rewarded for his restraint; he will in fact be penalized in competition with the over-exploiters. The commons of the oceanic fisheries is therefore inevitably headed for destruction because we have not yet seen how to bring the oceans under the regime of either socialism or privatism. However, the recent extension of the limit of national fishing rights out to 200 miles from shore is a partial step in the direction of national privatism (Hardin 1978b).

Much of the rapid "progress" of our commercial society has undoubtedly been made possible by externalizing many of the costs of enterprises. So-called externalities have shortened the lives of millions of miners and workers in industries mining or using asbestos, mercury and radioactive compounds. The automatic encouragement of innovation makes it difficult to internalize costs that take years to mature, e.g., the cost of cancers that do not appear until decades after exposure to carcinogens. Not until fifteen years ago, when the Ames test was developed, did we have a firm foundation for insisting on the internalization of the costs of a multitude of chemical industries (Ames 1979).

I think it would be possible to make a good case for the thesis that our present high level of material wealth could not have been reached--or at any rate, could not have been reached in a mere two centuries of time--without the externalizing of costs, without the grievous mistreating of workers that enabled technological evolution to proceed at the most rapid rate. In this historical sense, some people may feel that the injustice of imposed externalities in an unacknowledged commons was, in the long run, justified. I will not argue the point. But now that we have learned to identify the commons and their externalities it is most unlikely that we will permit this kind of "progress" to continue.

A Go-Go society, linked to externalities in its attempt to maximize "productivity," unthinkingly adopts the slogan of criminal law, "Innocent until proven guilty" (Hardin 1972). By contrast, the philosopher of a conserver society, recognizing that "we can never do merely one thing" (Hardin 1963), assumes that every proposed innovation carries with it a serious danger of causing unforeseen damage through its externalities; he therefore condemns the application of the ancient assumption to environmental matters, reversing it to read: "Guilty until proven innocent." With respect to proposed new drugs, this reversal was accomplished by the Kefauver-Harris Amendments to the Food, Drug and Cosmetics Act of 1962. Anyone who proposes to offer a new medicine for sale must now show that he has carried out *very* extensive tests to demonstrate that the drug does more good than harm; such tests may cost the enterpriser as much as ten million dollars before he can sell a single package. The principle of "Guilty until proven innocent" was also applied to environmental innovations by the National Environmental Policy Act beginning January 1, 1970. Environmental impact studies, expensive and time-consuming, must be carried out before any significant intervention in the environment is permitted (9).

Any analysis of the consequences of innovation made by a Go-Go society is very shallow, if it is made at all (10). A Go-Go addict does not want to know about externalities; such knowledge would slow up "progress." The conserver *does* want to know about them, because he is more interested in total effects, considered over both time and space. It is impossible to make any analysis really complete, and therefore the ecological viewpoint at times leads the conserver to make some rather murky statements. Since we cannot foresee *all* the consequences of any intervention throughout all time to infinity, we ultimately must compromise, drawing a line some place. But the line that is drawn by an ecologically minded conserver includes a much larger area of analysis than that used by a Go-Go enterpriser, whose area of analysis approximates to a mere point.

It follows that the amount of entrepreneurial activity in a Go-Go society is high (11), in contrast to that of a conserver society where it is low. It also follows that the rate of evolution of new commercial products is great in a Go-Go society. Since many new products are not very good the amount of waste involved in Go-Go is considerable. This is obvious to anyone who looks at the problem from the point of view of welfare economics, that is from the point of view of society as a whole. These wastes are not found in a conserver society, but we should not therefore relax our critical defenses. A sort of generalized extension of the second law of thermodynamics leads us to suspect that there is waste in every society. The waste of a new order of dealing with things will not for the most part be accurately known in advance. We should, therefore, look with suspicion on the most euphoric claims of those who praise and promote the conserver society, being alert for the new forms of waste that will no doubt turn up. We should take seriously the words of William Blake in his poem *Jerusalem* (1803):

> The hand of Vengeance sought the bed
> To which the purple tyrant fled;
> The iron hand crushed the tyrant's head.
> And became a tyrant in his stead.

Conservers who, in all innocence, intend only to save people from the tyranny of the incomplete accounting that characterized the old way of doing things should always keep in mind that *their* innovation--a new way of accounting--may generate a new tyranny. A physicist has warned us of this possibility in an article entitled "The Hidden Costs of Saying *NO*!" (Dyson 1975); hence the question mark entered on line 13 of Table 1. A biologist has contradicted the physicist by sarcastically extolling "The Benefits of Saying *YES*!" (Ehrlich 1975). The conflict between these two views is not easily resolved.

PSYCHOLOGICAL CONSEQUENCES OF THE CONSERVER MENTALITY

Our attitude toward the competing systems depends on where we stand: viewed from the Go-Go standpoint a Go-Go society is adventurous, a conserver society stodgy (14). Viewed from the other position the Go-Go society is frantic, the conserver society tranquil. Objectivity is not possible: "You pays your money and you takes your choice."

A Go-Go society is controlled (15) by market forces. (Externalities, by definition, lie outside of the control system.) A conserver society, by contrast, is almost bound to be controlled by bureaucracies, with all their dangers. Within its limited framework, the errors of a Go-Go society are well corrected (16) through economic loss and the failures of erring business enterprises. Errors of a conserver society require the detection of malfeasance by bureaucrats. Such detection is always difficult because the bureaucrats are likely also to control the sources of information and will make strenuous attempts to keep knowledge of their deficiencies from reaching the public who support them (Hardin and Baden 1977, p. 66). Within the limits set by the concept of "externalities" a Go-Go society deals more effectively with the information needed to correct errors.

Individuals (including the associations of individuals

called "firms") in a Go-Go society look out for their own interests by means of contracts. This leads to what Henry Maine called a "contract society" (17). It seems probable that a conserver society (by contrast), valuing safety above innovation, will multiply bureaucracies in its attempts to keep from making mistakes (thereby making mistakes of a different sort). Conservers will move toward the type of society that historically preceded the contract society, namely the "status society," with all of its advantages and disadvantages. Objectively (18) the people in a Go-Go society enjoy more freedom. Psychological freedom (19) is arguably a different matter. The philosopher Hegel said that "Freedom is the recognition of necessity." A person who recognizes the necessity of gravity, enjoys more psychological freedom than does the person who refuses to recognize this natural force, struggling continually and futilely against it. Similarly, when our theories of the politico-economic necessities are as firmly established as the theories of physics, by recognizing the necessities we will achieve greater psychological freedom than is possible for those who struggle against such recognition.

Perhaps the most revolutionary change implied by the transition from Go-Go to conservation is a change in our attitude toward advertising (20). In pointing this out we must make a distinction between advertising that has information as its goal and advertising that is concerned primarily with the competition between products that are essentially the same. As far as information is concerned it is easy to make a case for the position that there is public benefit to be derived from seeing to it that everybody knows what is available where and at what price. But modern advertising never stops at this point. From a public point of view it seldom makes the least difference whether the consumer buys Tweedledum Soap or Tweedledee Soap. An enterpriser who is well established in the market and confident of his competitive position may well be better off not advertising at all. Hershey candy bars are an example in point. By not advertising, the Hershey company avoids the waste of pulpwood trees used in newsprint, for instance. Competitive advertising is a "zero-sum game" as concerns the competitive makers of equivalent products, and a dead loss for society as a whole. But few enterprisers are as well established as the Hershey company, and so the waste of competitive advertising goes on and on.

As energy becomes scarcer, and conservation of resources more essential, we can expect some pressure to be put on the system of competitive advertising. However I think we can also doubt whether this pressure will be more than minimally effective. Bureaucrats try to control the information affecting their operations; so also will the wealthy advertising industry seek to control the expression of doubts of its social value. It is hard to conceive of a serious attack on, or even a serious examination of, advertising being made in a world in which economic control of the "media" is in the hands of the advertising industry. For the foreseeable future, the waste of competitive advertising will continue, unaltered by the transition from a Go-Go society to a conserver society. In fact, as the status aspects of societal organization become strengthened it may be that a significant reform of advertising will become all but impossible. But every society has to survive its own particular forms of waste, and perhaps the conserver society can survive this one.

WHAT WILL REMAIN UNCHANGED

Now that we have seen the major differences between the two types of society let us finish the analysis by giving a brief statement of the essential similarities between the two. (See Table 2.)

What has been called the Cardinal Rule of Policy (A) must be followed in both systems, if either is to work: "Never ask a person to act against his own self-interest" (Hardin 1977). The extent to which individuals may or may not be altruistic is still a disputed point, but we need not enter into this dispute here. Altruism, if it occurs, is a "marginal" activity, not one that we can build a politico-economic system on. It is one of the weaknesses of the present environmental movement that many of its spokesmen show a strong desire to control individuals or institutions by calling for altruistic self-sacrifice in the name of the whole of society. Calls for self-sacrifice are seldom answered, and for good reason. Those who answer such calls put themselves at a competitive disadvantage vis-a-vis non-altruists, and so are soon eliminated as socially effective forces.

The best basis for appealing to enterprisers is self-interest (B) and this basis is not altered by the change from a Go-Go society to a conserver society. What reformers must work for is a change in the rules that define self-interest, a change in the payoff of the game. An old Arab proverb says, "If the mice are eating you out of house and home, don't blame the mice--blame the mouse-hole." It is dangerous to fault people for responding to self-interest. If their actions produce results that are undesirable from the community's point of view it is up to the community to stop up the offending mouse-hole by changing the rules of the game.

Specifically (C) we can avoid the tragedy of the commons

only by putting an end to the commons. In a crowded world, tragedy is created whenever individual enterprisers, pursuing their own self-interest, degrade the world for everyone *including themselves*, as they do if they are allowed to throw unlimited wastes into the commons of air or water, or to catch fish without limit from the commons of the ocean. Since calling for altruism favors non-altruists, the proper approach is to get the exploiters of the commons to see how their long-term interest lies in getting rid of the commons, persuading the participants to follow a policy of "mutual coercion, mutually agreed upon" (Hardin 1968). However shocking some people may find this motto, it is merely an operational definition of *any* restrictive law passed by the majority in a democracy.

Finally, we must recognize that, whatever the system, competition can be a powerful conserver of excellence (D). It is perilous to create, or permit to continue, a system that does not allow competition. This is one of the dangers of the bureaucratic, status society into which we appear to be moving. A bureaucratic society needs some workable equivalent of the market forces that prevail in a contract society. It should look for ways of creating competition between bureaus, or ways of preserving some contract elements in an essentially bureaucratic society. One solution that we have already stumbled upon is what has been called the "grants economy." In this system, the government, instead of supporting a monolithic bureau to do a certain job, writes contracts with independent agencies to do so--competitively. Whatever waste is inherent in competition of this sort is more than made up for by the excellence that can result from people competing under contract. At any rate, this is the sort of thing that we should look for in our creative examination of the possibilities of surviving under the rigors of a conserver society, which is the only society rationally open to us once we *know* that we live in a limited world.

TABLE 2. SOME THINGS THAT WILL BE UNCHANGED

A. The Cardinal Rule of Policy:
   Never ask a person to act against his own self-interest.

B. Best basis for appealing to enterprisers and managers:
   Self-interest.

C. Method of avoiding "tragedy of the commons":
   Mutual coercion, mutually agreed upon.

D. Competition a powerful conserver of excellence.

REFERENCES

Ames, Bruce N. (1979), "Identifying Environmental Chemicals Causing Mutations and Cancer," *Science*, 204,587-593.

Brooks, John (1973), *The Go-Go Years*, New York: Weybright and Talley.

Dyson, Freeman J. (1975), "The Hidden Costs of Saying *NO!*," *Bulletin of the Atomic Scientists*, 31(6):23-27.

Ehrlich, Paul R. (1975), "The Benefits of Saying *YES!*," *Bulletin of the Atomic Scientists*, 31(7):49-51.

Hardin, Garrett (1963), "The Cybernetics of Competition," *Perspectives in Biology and Medicine*, 7,58-84.

_____, (1968), "The Tragedy of the Commons," *Science*, 162, 1243-1248.

_____, (1969), "The Economics of Wilderness," *Natural History*, 78(6):20-27. [Reprinted in Hardin 1978a]

_____, (1972), *Exploring New Ethics for Survival: The Voyage of the Spaceship Beagle*, New York: Viking.

_____, (1977), *The Limits of Altruism*, Bloomington: Indiana University Press.

_____, (1978a), *Stalking the Wild Taboo*, 2nd edition, Los Altos, Calif.: Kaufmann.

_____, (1978b), "Political Requirements for Preserving Our Common Heritage," *Wildlife and America*, Howard P. Brokaw, editor, Washington, D.C.: Council on Environmental Quality.

_____, and John Baden, (1977), *Managing the Commons*, San Francisco: Freeman.

Pigou, A.C. (1920), *The Economics of Welfare*, London: Macmillan.

Schumacher, E.F. (1973), *Small is Beautiful*, New York: Harper Torchbooks.

Sparrow, John (1977), *Too Much of a Good Thing*, Chicago: University of Chicago Press.

Veblen, Thorstein (1899), *The Theory of the Leisure Class*, New York: Macmillan.

SCARCITY AS AN INTELLECTUAL RESOURCE:
NOTES ON THE TECHNOLOGY OF A CONSERVER SOCIETY

Douglas M. Costle
U.S. Environmental Protection Agency
Washington, D.C.

THE PRICE OF KNOWLEDGE

According to Greek myth, the most skilled craftsman of the ancient world was the architect and sculptor Daedalus. Among other achievements, Daedalus is credited with having built the labyrinth for King Minos on the island of Crete.

Sometime after that, however, Daedalus fell out of favor with King Minos, and was forced to devise a means of escape for himself and his son, Icarus. This he did by fashioning wings, out of feathers and wax.

The wings worked perfectly -- but human judgment did not. In his pride at being able to soar through the air, Icarus flew too close to the sun -- and the wax fastening his wings to his body melted. Icarus plunged to his death in the sea.

Perhaps if there had been a Consumer Product Safety Commission at the time, or an Aegean Aviation Administration, this tragedy might have been averted. Icarus would have been required to make several training flights before launching himself over water, and the wings themselves might have been stamped with a label reading: "CAUTION: EXCESSIVE HEAT MAY ABRUPTLY TERMINATE YOUR FLIGHT."

Neither of those regulatory mechanisms existed at the time, of course, so all we are left with is an interesting tale. But so often these ancient myths -- like Aesop's fables, or the parables of the New Testament -- clothe a provocative truth or profound question in story form. And it is intriguing to note how many of those stories, old and new, ask the same question as that posed by the story of Daedalus and his son.

What is the price we pay for knowledge? By taking a bite out of that apple, Adam could suddenly distinguish between good and evil; was that gain worth the loss of the Garden of Eden? Prometheus stole fire, the beginning of civilization, from Zeus, and brought it to mankind; was that gift worth the plagues from Pandora's Box that Zeus sent as punishment? The technology created by Daedalus killed his son; was it worth it?

Dr. Faustus traded his soul for a command of science and the companionship of Helen of Troy -- giving us not only an allegory, but an adjective: a few years back, Dr. Alvin Weinberg, then director of the Oak Ridge National Laboratory, referred to man's harnessing of nuclear power as "a Faustean bargain. . ."

MODERN COUNTERPART

Thus this theme of man's paying a heavy price for knowledge and comfort echoes down through the ages. It is echoing today, in the wake of our near-miss with Three Mile Island.

Three Mile Island is still fresh in our minds, and so our questions about man's control of the technology he has created tend to emphasize nuclear problems. In point of fact, however, the last few years have surfaced questions about an extraordinary variety of our technologies. Today's headlines, in this era of almost instantaneous communication, can lead us to forget yesterday's -- and, perhaps, distract us from noting a pattern that apparently isolated events suggest.

Yesterday's headline, for example, chronicled the fiery descent of Skylab -- fortunately, in a sparsely populated area of Australia. Before that, we read about the blow-out of an offshore drilling rig in Mexico's Bay of Campeche, which swiftly became the largest oil-spill in world history. The headline before that told us about the Love Canal, in Niagara Falls, New York; in only a few months, that tragically named ditch became a generic term for a host of chemical time-bombs in virtually every state of the Union, ticking their way toward sudden trouble in tempo with an unknown clock. Before that, we had Kepone, and before that, we read of thousands of cattle in Michigan being systematically slaughtered and buried because a toxic, fire-retardant chemical named PBB had mistakenly been mixed in with their feed.

Furthermore, these single, attention-getting events unfold against a background of continuing dangers that rarely generate news because they are "happening" 365 days a year -- not only in the United States, but across the globe:

> Scientists in most of the industrialized First World nations, as well as their colleagues in the Soviet Union, have begun to monitor "acid rains" -- dilute sulfuric and nitric acid falling hundreds of miles away from the factories that generated the emissions. It has been demonstrated that these rains lower soil productivity and reduce timber production.

In April, 1978, the U.S. imposed a ban on interstate shipment of convenience products that use chlorofluorocarbons as propellants; it is believed that CFCs can rise into the atmosphere, decompose under the influence of sunlight, and erode the ozone that protects humans, animals, and crops from ultraviolet radiation. Sweden started phasing out CFC aerosols two months later, Canada began developing regulations on them, and the Netherlands imposed a requirement for warning labels.

And while scientists warn about the possible consequences of a carbon dioxide build-up in the atmosphere -- a "greenhouse effect" that might produce a disastrous rise in global temperatures and some melting of the polar ice-cap -- all of us, including the Third World nations, continue to increase our burning of fossil fuels.

These noteworthy examples might well induce gloom about the future of our global environment and man's ability to manage it so that natural systems will sustain our species for the indefinite future. Yet some events -- notably the astonishingly swift growth of an environmental awareness around the globe, and mounting interest in the concept of a "Conserver Society" -- offer solid reason for hope.

TECHNOLOGY AND LIMITS

We have begun to recognize that man's technology, coupled with his numbers on the planet, have brought us to a genuine turning-point in our three-million-year long history. That turning-point has already begun to make some differences in the way we live, and will unquestionably force more drastic changes in the future.

But the necessity for such changes need not return us to a Dark Ages of human comfort or spirit. On the contrary, it can provide a new direction for human innovation. Instead of being intimidated or diminished by our growing sense of limits on human activities, we can learn to use that sense as an intellectual stimulus.

Clearly technology -- wasteful as it often is -- has given us social and personal benefits too numerous and too obvious to mention.

Further, problems with technology are not new; 19th century history is an unending chronicle of industrial and mari-

time disasters -- not to mention the epidemic diseases which our
ancestors accepted as inevitable. And as Thomas Hobbes pointed
out two centuries earlier, the life of man in a state of nature
is not a pastoral dream; it is "nasty, brutish, and short,"
characterized by "continual fear and danger of violent death."

Implications of Limits

What *is* new about the problems our technologies create is
the potential they pose for massive damage, and the fact that
so many of them -- from nuclear waste to energy depletion --
are suddenly **converging** on us at the same time. It is this combination of technological scale and technological convergence --
both of them magnified by population increase -- that is the
essence of a turning point in man's history. Simply expressed,
we have come within sight of the limits of our planet's capacity
to sustain past rates of growth in human demand on finite resources.

I will not try here to defend that statement. It is obvious in the case of some resources, such as oil -- and less
obvious but equally true in the case of others, such as water.
In any case, the "limits to growth" argument has been pro-
pounded by wiser people than I; the debate tends to be not so
much about the fact of limits to growth, as about the timing:
when will it arrive?

Rather than offer my own guess, I would prefer to discuss
some of the implications that a limit on growth holds for us.
Equally important, I would like to discuss some implications
that it does not have.

For one thing, the term "limits on growth" refers to only
certain kinds of growth: population growth for one, growth in
consumption of finite physical resources for another.

It need not refer to limits on economic growth. We have
become so accustomed to equating growth in our economy with
growth in consumption that we assume one cannot continue without the other. But to choose a homely example, if a furniture
manufacturer can figure out how to carve five chairs out of a
tree when he used to get four, he will realize a 25 percent
gain in output with no increase in input -- none, that is,
except brains.

Lest this be considered a fanciful, unattainable prospect,
let me mention how a sense of limits has already stimulated innovation and economic growth in the environmental control field.

Innovation in Environmental Control

Broadly speaking, a manufacturer has two ways of **complying**

19

with anti-pollution laws. He can collect his garbage in a big pail when it pours out the end of the factory pipe; or he can improve what goes on <u>inside</u> the factory, so that his process generates less garbage to begin with. Either strategy costs money -- but the second, which requires ingenuity as well as money, can pay dividends.

Here are some examples of such ingenuity:

> An $8 million water treatment system installed by Great Lakes Paper Company reduced overall plant operating costs by $4 million a year; in three years, therefore, the system will not only have paid for itself, but will have started producing profits.

> A refuse plant on Boston's North Shore burns 438,000 tons of garbage a year, providing local industry with steam equal in energy value to 27 million gallons of fuel oil.

> Air burners installed at a Florida Power Corporation generating plant to reduce particulate emissions not only comply with clean air standards, but save the company 4,000 barrels of oil a year.

> Solid waste incinerators at the John Deere works in Dubuque burn waste to generate steam heat for the factory, saving about $1,175 a day in waste disposal and fuel costs.

> By redesigning manufacturing processes, the 3M Company in Minneapolis has cut the equivalent of 73,000 tons of air pollutants and 500 million gallons of wastewater annually, and saved about $11 million in actual or deferred costs.

INCENTIVES FOR INNOVATION

None of these innovations originated spontaneously; they were triggered by environmental regulation -- a negative incentive of imposed controls backed up by fines for failure to comply. Nevertheless, once these companies looked at their regulatory problems in a fresh light, they all made money on their creativity. As one glass manufacturer testified, after realizing a 10 percent savings in energy costs and boosting production to an all-time high, "If EPA hadn't put the squeeze on us, none of this would have happened."

If the negative incentive of government compulsion -- some

federal agency "putting the squeeze on" -- could stimulate so much creativity, so much innovation, could not positive incentive -- the unforced perception of possible gain -- stimulate several times more?

We have not lost our capacity to invent. Rather, those who believe that an "Age of Limits" forecloses future discovery and growth cling to the ghosts of past inventions, failing to recognize that we live in a genuinely new age -- one that requires not merely improving familiar technologies, but new technologies entirely.

Some time after the achievement of the first successful chain reaction in an atomic pile at the University of Chicago, Albert Einstein remarked, "Everything has changed -- except the way we think."

Man's need to respect the limits of his globe does not necessarily point us down a gloomy road to a cold, joyless existence. On the contrary, it invites us to change the way we think. Like all our familiar resources -- timber, land, fossil fuels, our air, water, and soil -- so the perception of physical limit, the recognition of scarcity, can itself be a resource. It can be an intellectual resource that points our technology in a new direction: toward a fresh, infinitely more creative mode of invention that keeps human demand in balance with the earth's supply.

The outlines of some of those technologies are already clear to us -- and so are the carrots, the rewards, the <u>positive</u> incentives:

>A fortune awaits the first person or the first company to produce a cheap photovoltaic cell, capable of transforming sunlight to electricity.
>
>A fortune awaits those who -- employing the concept of scarcity as an intellectual resource -- figure out how to make the recycling of household wastes economically feasible.
>
>Conservation is commonly viewed as a process of doing without; enormous rewards await those who perceive that conservation means making the same amount of resources produce more -- and who can convert that perception into industrial specifics that will be applauded by both the Sierra Club and Dow-Jones.

The point is that man's new relationship to his technology does not foreclose the opportunity for invention; rather, it opens up opportunities for a new _type_ of invention.

NEW WINGS

Technology has lifted us, like Icarus, into the middle air -- proud of our flight, exulting in our power, and tempted to test that power by flying toward the sun. Seduced by the illusion of our own omnipotence, we can fly too close -- and fall to our end.

But while we ponder the cautionary example of Icarus, we should also remember Daedalus. It was he, after all, who invented the wings in the first place. He knew that innovation requires courage -- but he also knew that courage is not the same thing as bravado, and that risk is not the same thing as foolishness. By blending imagination and daring with a sense of limits, Daedalus concluded his flight safely.

And so, if we scale our new technologies to the perception of limits, can we. Resource constraints need not ground us; only the intellectual ceilings we place on ourselves can do that. A whole sky -- unsullied, unexplored, and infinitely promising -- awaits us. All we need to take possession of this fresh freedom, and escape from our insular bondage in the technological servitude of the past, is some new wings.

CANADA'S CONSERVER SOCIETY STUDIES: THEIR INTELLECTUAL AND SOCIAL IMPACT[1]

Stanley J. Shapiro, McGill University, Montreal

The concept of a conserver society is a Canadian export available free of charge to all those looking for a new approach in a world confronted with shortages, scarcities and limits of all types. That an American Marketing Association Workshop would devote itself to further explorations of this Canadian concept is an especially gratifying development. The first Ecological Marketing Workshop contributed immeasurably to my understanding of the marketing dimensions of a conserver society (Henion and Kinnear 1976). Its impact is clearly reflected in the background paper I subsequently prepared on that subject (Shapiro 1976). Hopefully, the current meeting will generate a good many further insights into both the immediate area of concern -- marketing in a conserver society -- and the more generic problem of ecological marketing.

This paper briefly reviews Canada's two benchmark Conserver Society studies. Major emphasis is placed, however, on the political, economic, social and intellectual "fall out" associated with these two projects. More specifically, attention will be focussed on the degree of media coverage received by the Conserver Society studies; the follow-up articles written and the innumerable speeches made by Conserver Society researchers; the business response; the public policy impact; the related research now underway; and other Canadian publications that should be of interest to those seriously exploring the Conserver Society concept.

Though the author believes this undertaking is a worthwhile one, he also realizes its limitations. First, the two Conserver Society reports were not the only scarcity, shortage or ecological crisis literature to have had a major impact on Canadian thinking. The growth controversy has become the major intellectual concern of the 1970's with the Conserver Society accounting for only a small proportion of the relevant material. Similarly, it is difficult to determine the relative importance in affecting behaviour of Conserver Society discussions and

---

[1] The author wishes to acknowledge the assistance and helpful comments provided by John Coleman of CTV, Dr. Arthur Cordell and Dr. Ray Jackson of the Science Council of Canada, Trevor Hancock, M.D. of the National Survival Institute and Dr. Kimon Valaskakis of GAMMA and the University of Montreal.

"limits to growth" debates vis-à-vis the resource shortages that have existed and the price increases that have occurred since OPEC became an effective force. Finally, the information available on the direct impact of the two conserver society studies -- even when viewed in isolation from other literature and from actual resource shortages -- has proven to be inadequate and incomplete. This review, therefore, is advanced as a tentative and far from exhaustive effort. References, insights and observations provided by a wide variety of individuals and organizations have been relied upon in an attempt to sketch the "societal fallout" of Canada's Conserver Society studies.

WHAT IS A CONSERVER SOCIETY?

What are we talking about when we talk about a conserver society? This is an obvious question to ask but not an especially easy one to answer. There are at least three levels of definition or meaning associated with the term. First, there is the operational definition advanced by the Science Council of Canada (1976a).

> The concept of a conserver society arises from a deep concern for the future and the realization that decisions taken today in such areas as energy and nonrenewable resources, for example, may have an irreversible and possibly destructive impact in the medium to long term.
>
> The necessity for a conserver society derives from our perception of the world as finite and of nonrenewable resources as limited, as well as from our recognition of increasing global interdependence.
>
> A conserver society is, on principle, against waste. Therefore, it is a society which
>
> promotes economy of design of all systems, i.e., "doing more with less";
>
> favors reuse or recycling, and wherever possible, reduction at the source;
>
> questions the ever-growing per capita demand for consumer goods artifically encouraged by modern marketing techniques; and
>
> recognizes that a diversity of solutions in many systems, such as energy and transportation, might in effect increase their overall economy, stability, and

resiliency.

In a conserver society, the pricing mechanism should not just reflect the private cost, but rather should reflect the total cost to society, including net energy used, ecological impact, and social considerations. This will permit the market system to allocate resources in a manner that more closely reflects societal needs, both immediate and long term.

A broader guage definition of the "conserver society" requires equating such a society with the nature and scope of either or both of the two benchmark studies conducted by the Science Council of Canada and the Group Associé Montréal/McGill pour l'etude de l'avenir (GAMMA). The summary statement found in Exhibit 1 provides a feel for the scope of the Science Council study. That entire report, of course, is "must reading" in any examination of the ecological impact of modern marketing (Science Council of Canada 1977). The integrating GAMMA volume, The Selective Conserver Society, also makes a strong case for conservation (Valaskakis et al. 1977a). Its most unique features are the emphasis on limiting not "growth" but negative forward throughput and the contrasting of three proposed policy options--CS_1 or doing more with less, CS_2 or doing the same with less, CS_3 or doing less with less--with the status quo (CS_0) and the "squander society" (CS_{-1}). A summary treatment of the integrating GAMMA report prepared by its authors has been published in Planning Review (Valaskakis et al. 1977b). That article is the source of Exhibit 2 which compares the five societal prototypes along a number of key dimensions. Exhibit 3 operationalizes the concept of negative forward throughput.

EXHIBIT 1

CANADA AS A CONSERVER SOCIETY --
A SUMMARY OF SCIENCE COUNCIL STUDY NO. 27

The Report questions the way in which our society has chosen to transform resources into commodities, and the ways Canadians have become accustomed to a way of life that involves high rates of resource use, high waste, and constantly inflating expectations. Symptoms of environmental and social stress indicate that a transition must begin toward more sustainable and selective patterns of growth.

Five basic initiatives or thrusts characterize policy that will help us make a smooth transition to a conserver society: concern for the future, economy of design, attention to diversity and flexibility, recognition of total costs, and respect for the regenerative capacity of the biosphere.

The planning of individuals, business and government must develop a sense of direction and lengthened perspectives to ensure that we keep options open.

We must strive not simply to react to crises and shortages but to attain greater flexibility and efficiency, the elimination of wasteful practices, and the re-orientation of our expectations.

Diversity in human activities, as in natural ecological systems, increases flexibility, adaptability and resiliency. It allows the decentralization of responsibility and the optimization of performance from local resources.

If the true costs of our activities - to others, to ourselves, and to future populations - could be seen for what they are, a conserver society would be an almost automatic result.

A constant aim of the conserver viewpoint is techno-socio-economic processes that are in principle sustainable and self-renewing and that do not overload the capacity of the biosphere to assimilate waste.

Energy supply is becoming a primary constraint on our present pattern of growth; the difficulty and expense of bringing new sources of supply on line have made measures to improve the efficiency with which we use energy and measures to conserve energy very appealing. The application of conserver principles will give us invaluable flexibility and manoeuvring space as we go through the transition away from fossil fuels.

One aim of the conserver society will be to achieve, over the long term, reliance on sources of energy which are in principle sustainable. This will mean a preference for renewable energy sources, such as hydro, solar, wind and vegetation, in contrast with present policies in the industrialized countries of maintaining high standards of living at the expense of non-replaceable fossil fuels.

From a conserver point of view, we would be better off to pay more attention to materials, not as throughput or flow, but as "stock," fixed in the form of buildings, roads, etc. and circulating in the form of new investment, depreciation, recycling, consumption and disposal. The ultimate goal will be a change from a system of high extraction, high flow and high disposal with recycling a minor component, to a system in which optimum use is made of a fixed and recycling stock, with new extraction necessary only for growth and "topping-up" as materials degrade from wear, tear and mixing.

A conserver approach will create new technologies, new opportunities for Canadian business and unprecedented challenges for the entrepreneurial spirit. The new "conserver" wave of industrialization, already underway, is based on the need for new energy sources, greater efficiency in energy use, miniaturization, process control technology, and new technologies based on ecological science.

Among urgent priorities, the Report recommends that the transportation and residential building sectors become vastly more energy efficient; and that steps be taken to stimulate the development of Canadian renewable energy technologies, to improve the ways we manage and use materials, and to promote new industries and employment opportunities compatible with the conserver approach.

Source: Extracted from a summary description of <u>Canada as a Conserver Society: Resource Uncertainties and the Need for New Technologies</u> (Ottawa: Science Council of Canada, 1977).

Finally, the term "Conserver Society" is often employed by Canadians in an even more far-reaching sense. Such a society is being advocated by environmentalists, ecologists, Club of Rome supporters, advocates of social reform, opponents of mass advertising and by many others as a highly desirable alternative to the prevailing trinity -- economic growth, mass consumption and affluence. For these individuals, the conserver society is viewed not only as a goal or social objective that is ecologically necessary but, in addition, as an attractive and appealing option in its own right.

EXHIBIT 2

A COMPARISON OF THE CONSUMER AND CONSERVER SOCIETIES

	The Selective Conserver Society			*Consumer Alternatives*	
	CS_1	CS_2	CS_3	CS_0	CS_{-1}
	Efficiency Scenario	High Stable State	"Buddhist" Society	Status Quo	Squander Society
Thematic description	Doing more with less	Doing the same with less	Doing less with less	Doing more with more	Doing less with more
Goal	Seek maximization of felicity by minimizing waste, living in harmony with nature, and keeping options open for the future.			Seeking maximization of felicity without the constraints of conservation.	
General objective	Efficiency	Industrial stability	Nonindustrial stability	Growth	
Specific objectives	Reduce waste without changing values	Freeze demand at optimum level	Reduce demand	Mixed laissez-faire	Increase demand

27

EXHIBIT 2 CONT'D.

Principal strategies	Rental schemes, RICH, Tech. change, Full cost-pricing public regulation	Demarketing, evenhanded advertising, education	Education, demonstration of attractiveness of option	Mixed laissez-faire	Consumer sovereignty
Possible impact on inflation	Uncertain	Uncertain, probably antiinflationary	Probably antiinflationary	Inflationary	Very inflationary
Possible impact on unemployment	Reduces unproductive employment, increases productive	Uncertain	Create employment	High unemployment	Very low unemployment
Population policy	Zero growth, excluding immigration unless otherwise shown	Zero growth, excluding immigration unless otherwise shown	Zero growth, excluding immigration unless otherwise shown	No definitive policy	No definitive policy
Implications concerning growth in forward throughput	Controlled growth in forward throughput matched by growth in reverse throughput	Zero growth in forward throughput	Reduction of existing forward throughput	High growth in forward throughput with very little recycling	Higher growth in forward throughput and no recycling
Possible impact on income distribution	Tendency toward egalitarian distribution	Very egalitarian	Egalitarian	Perpetuates income inequalities	Increases income inequalities
Possible impact on balance of payments	Uncertain	Probably improves B/P	Probably improves B/P	Worsens B/P	Worsens B/P
Impact on life-styles	Behavior changes but not values	Some change in values	Radical change in values and life-styles	Existing life-style	More wasteful practices

Source: Valaskakis et al. "The Conserver Society," *Planning Review*, September, 1977, p. 19.

EXHIBIT 3

THE LIMITS TO THROUGHPUT

The input limits to throughput:

1. The depletion threat of nonrenewable and renewable resources. It is intuitively clear that it is possible to deplete nonrenewables, but it is less obvious concerning renewables. However, we can also "overload" a "renewable" water system by polluting it so severely that we destroy the natural mechanisms of self-renewal.

2. High extraction costs in money terms. The extraction of raw materials from the soil or the earth's crust is a costly process. The sheer economics of extraction may be an effective limit to further throughput.

3. High extraction costs in energy terms. Money cost does not always reflect total cost. In some instances a more meaningful measure is energy cost - the energy cost of extracting a barrel of crude from the Alberta tar sands vs.

extraction in Saudi Arabia.

4. High extraction cost in environmental terms. Notwithstanding the two measures of extraction cost, there is a further input limit in terms of environmental deterioration. Certain extraction techniques gravely disturb the environment.

The output limits to throughput:

5. Intended output threatens the environment. This situation occurs where geographical concentration of industrial activity, causing high-density urbanization, leads to environmental deterioration. Urban sprawl robs the land of alternative uses and, in addition, may create certain critical chemical imbalances in the atmosphere.

6. Unintended output of production throughput threatens environment. This category covers the general effluents and by-products of the productive process (scrap, waste, air pollution, noise, poisons).

7. Unintended output of consumption throughput threatens environment. Here lies an important limit: postconsumer waste. The consumer destroys the product in the process of consumption and produces garbage, noxious gases, noise, and/or pollution.

The subjective limits to throughput:

8. Institutional limits to throughput. Functional imperfections of social institutions are both effects and causes of throughput. These problems include the inability of the market to price all costs, the failure of the communication network to provide adequate advance warning of dangers, and the limited absorptive capacity of institutions.

9. Value limits and "other." In this category lie the value dimensions which, depending on culture and personality, are either favorable or inimical to high throughput. The value system imposes a constraint upon the absorptive capacity of institutions.

10. Human-health limits. The human body maintains homeostasis by keeping within fairly narrow limits such life indicators as heartbeat, brain waves and blood pressure. Throughput, as a process which is intended to provide for human needs, must be of the type and quantity which in fact serves and does not frustrate that purpose.

Source: Valaskakis et al., 1979, Harper & Row, pp. 39-41.

PUBLICITY -- FROM FIRST (ALMOST) TO LAST

Both Conserver Society studies were well underway but attracting relatively little public attention until then Prime Minister Trudeau, in a New Year's greeting for 1976, questioned the adequacy of the market mechanism as a regulatory device and the appropriateness of mass consumption as a dominant societal objective. These remarks were made some two and one-half months after the Trudeau government had introduced price and wage controls. They were interpreted by a nervous business community as revealing the direction in which that government proposed to move after the period of controls had come to an end. The publicity surrounding the original Trudeau statement and a "clarifying" speech made a few weeks later focussed attention on the two conserver society studies. The research teams came to be viewed -- in some circles at least -- as working on prototypes of what Trudeau had in mind.

Media attention was the rule rather than the exception during 1976 and 1977. The Science Council's Statement of Concern, issued in February of 1976, was deliberately intended to invite debate, discussion and response (1976b). GAMMA submitted a final report to its government sponsors during the summer of 1976 and scheduled a press conference on that report a few months later. The final Science Council Report was issued in September of 1977. All three of these submissions attracted considerable cross-Canada press coverage. In addition, Science Council personnel and GAMMA researchers were featured speakers during the 1976-78 period at over 200 public meetings, conferences, workshops, debates, forums and the like. Many of these speeches, in turn, also attracted considerable press coverage, though usually on a local level.

Nor were GAMMA and the Science Council immune from criticism and controversy. Publication of the Statement of Concern in Science Forum in early 1976 generated some critical letters to the editor, which were, in turn, answered by Science Council staff members (Science Forum 1976). GAMMA was some months later criticized by a nationally syndicated newspaper columnist whose charges generated a Science Council letter to the editor that was published in Ottawa and a countervailing column by GAMMA's director that appeared in The Montreal Star. Indeed, the Conserver Society has remained newsworthy for close to four years even though Canada has been plagued all during that same period by inflation, unemployment and separatist agitation.

The Conserver Society also became the subject of feature sections or special issues of a number of widely distributed

Canadian periodicals. Some of these magazines are referenced in Exhibit 4. That the Conserver Society also has its own special interest journal is also revealed. Conserver Society Notes is now a privately published periodical though its genesis was a newsletter distributed by the Science Council. Each issue of this quarterly contains a variety of articles relevant to one or more aspects of a conserver society. The same exhibit reveals that a number of other articles by Canadian authors on Conserver Society themes have appeared in North American journals and business practitioner publications. Also listed in Exhibit 4 are the "popular version" of the GAMMA summary report published in 1979 by Harper and Row, another book length treatment of The Conserver Solution and the widely disseminated Proceedings of the 1978 Couchiching Conference, Canada's most prestigious forum for public discussion.

EXHIBIT 4

RELEVANT "FOLLOW-UP" LITERATURE

I. Special Magazine Features

1. Canadian Consumer (June 1966)
2. Environment News - (Published by the Government of Alberta - Jan.-Feb. 1977)
3. Perception: A Canadian Journal of Social Comment (May-June 1978)
4. Saturday Night (March 1977)
5. The New Conserver Society Notes: Canada's Leading Magazine in the War on Waste. Must reading for a wide variety of relevant articles. Published by Alternatives, Inc., P.O. Box 2097, Station C, Downsview, Ontario, M3N 2S8. Subscriptions to this quarterly are $5.00 a year.

II. Related Articles

1. The New Conserver Society Notes (1978), "Canada as a Conserver Society: An Agenda for Action," (Summer), 4-15.
2. Paehlke, Robert (1978), "Canada: toward a Conserver Society," Environment, (April), 4-6.
3. Shapiro, Stanley J. (1978), "Marketing in a Conserver Society," Business Horizons, (April), 3-13.
4. Smith, J.G. (1978), "Conservationist Growth: An Opportunity for Canadian Business?" Business Quarterly, (Winter), 20-27.

5. Smith, J.G. (1978), "A Conserver Society: Some Implications for the Packaging Industry," Planning Review, (July), 10-13.

6. Stapenhurst, Frederick (1977), "Some Implications of a Conserver Society," Labour Gazette, (November), 511-513.

7. Stimulus (1978), "Advertising and the Conserver Society," (May-June), 23-25.

III. Books

1. Solomon, Lawrence (1978), The Conserver Solution, Toronto: Doubleday.

2. Valaskakis, Kimon, Peter S. Sindell, J. Graham Smith, Iris Fitzpatrick-Martin (1979), The Conserver Society: A Workable Alternative for the Future, New York: Harper & Row.

3. Walker, Dean, ed. (1979), Growth in a Conserving Society - The 47th Couchiching Conference, Toronto: Canadian Institute on Public Affairs.

Nearly four years have passed since Prime Minister Trudeau's New Year's message for 1976. The Conserver Society concept has moved during that period from an intellectual construct being explored in rarified circles to the most frequently discussed Canadian response to the ecological crisis. Benchmark reports, press coverage of these reports, mass media feature stories, subsequent follow-up articles, speeches and conferences -- all these factors and other developments discussed below have contributed to incredibly widespread dissemination of the Conserver Society concept.

THE CORPORATE REACTION

The Conserver Society has been taken very seriously by Canada's business community in general and by its marketing fraternity in particular. A number of leading trade associations such as the Association of Canadian Advertisers, The Institute of Canadian Advertising (the agency trade association), the Canadian Advertising Advisory Board (charged with self-regulation of the industry), the Retail Council of Canada and the Grocery Manufacturers' Association of Canada have sponsored at least one seminar or convention program on the Conserver Society. Business representatives have also participated in a number of public seminars and some corporations have formally reviewed the Conserver Society studies with their senior managers. The most significant business response, however, was the gradual evolution of the Alpha group, an umbrella organization of trade associations originally established for another purpose, into a quasi-official coordinating force for corporate discussion and the dissemination of information about the Conserver Society.

With a few noteworthy exceptions, the initial business response to the Conserver Society was a negative one. Once more, it was argued, the Canadian government proposed to encroach on Canada's increasingly constricted market economy. The previously mentioned introduction of wage, price and dividend controls and Mr. Trudeau's well publicized New Year's message contributed greatly to that feeling. The steadily growing antipathy between business and government associated with the increased degree of government regulation introduced during the late 1960's and early 1970's also helps to explain an almost automatic initial rejection. Interestingly enough, subsequent reflection within the business community has generated a certain amount of intellectual support for the conserver position. There is also growing recognition of the fact that the adoption of conserver values and conserver practices would create new markets and offer challenging opportunities in many different areas of economic activity.

THE RESPONSE OF GOVERNMENT

The Federal government of Prime Minister Trudeau never publicly endorsed the concept of Canada's becoming a Conserver Society. As far as can be determined, both Canada's elected politicians and the nation's senior civil servants have been divided as to the relative desirability of such a society. In any case, problems of inflation, unemployment and national unity soon became dominant government priorities. The position of Canada's newly elected Progressive Conservative government toward the Conserver Society remains, at time of writing, to be determined.

Energy conservation has been accepted as both a federal and a provincial priority. Studies of the likely economic impact of efforts at energy conservation have helped alleviate the fear that a Conserver Society would, per se and of necessity, generate a higher level of involuntary unemployment. It now appears that less energy intensive approaches to manufacturing would, on balance, create jobs rather than destroy them. The Science Council of Canada has been especially active in promoting research on the compatibility of employment and energy conservation.

One federal government agency has consciously encouraged further discussion of the Conserver Society. The Ministry of

State for Science and Technology sponsored five regional workshops that took place in February, March and April of 1978. The central concern of these workshops and the source documents presented on each occasion appear in Exhibit 5. Copies of the summary document containing all of these reports have recently become available (Ministry of State 1979). Many of the workshop presentations advanced conserver society thinking to a level of specificity considerably beyond that found in the GAMMA and Science Council studies.

What degree of public acceptance and legislative support is a Conserver Society likely to gain? Shortages and rising energy prices have already encouraged legislative action along this one dimension of the conserver society. However, it remains to be seen whether Canadian society will reach a social consensus regarding the doing of "less with less", "the same with less" or even "more with less" which will subsequently be reflected in both law and public policy. A useful model for evaluating the likely degree of Conserver Society acceptance is advanced by Molitar in his study of how other proposed changes in social and public policy have gained both widespread support and legislative embodiment (1977).

EXHIBIT 5

PAPERS PRESENTED AT THE VARIOUS MINISTRY
OF STATE CONSERVER SOCIETY WORKSHOPS

Atlantic Regional Workshop - Renewable Energy

1. Canadian Renewable Energy Prospects
2. Renewable Energy Sources: Operational Examples
3. Institutional Factors
4. Energy Conservation - Means and Ends

Prairie Regional Workshop - The Technological Challenge for Small Communities

1. Characteristics of Prairie Communities
2. Technological Change in Food Production and Processing in the Prairie Provinces
3. Water and Waste Management - Small Prairie Communities
4. Energy and the Conserver Society on the Prairies

Pacific Regional Workshop - Recycling and Solid Waste Management

1. Some Potential Strategies for the Recovery and Reduction of Municipal Waste
2. Wood Wastes as an Energy Source for the B.C. Pulp and Paper Industry: Economic Implications and Institutional Barriers

3. Energy from Waste in the Forest Products Industry
4. Solids Waste Handling in the Fish Processing Industry
5. Recycling and Solid Waste Management in the Fruit and Vegetables Industry
6. Overcoming Obstacles to the Conserver Society: The Individual, the Institution and the Co-op

Ontario Regional Workshop - Business and Industry in a Conserving Society

1. Some Impacts of the Conserver Society on Canadian Business
2. Impacts of Conserverism - The Marketing Perspective
3. The Conserver Society and the New Economics
4. The Conserver Society - Beginning the Dialogue

Quebec Regional Workshop - Industrial Opportunities in a Conserving Society

1. Appropriate Technologies as Opportunities for Development
2. Economic and Conservationist Objectives are Compatible
3. Communications and Information Process: Challenges and Opportunities for Canada
4. Potential for Industrial Development in the Conserver Society - Institutional Implications

Source: The Conserver Society: The Technological Challenge: Background Papers, (Ottawa, Ministry of State for Science and Technology, 1979).

GAMMA SPIN-OFF STUDIES

In accordance with long accepted and widely venerated academic tradition, the GAMMA study generated proposals for a series of follow-up investigations. To date, three such studies have been undertaken by GAMMA team members though none of them in the form in which they were originally proposed. GAMMA has become increasingly interested in the social and technological impact of our emerging Information Society. The conserver implications of such a society are major concerns of a research effort funded primarily by the federal Department of Communication (Valaskakis 1979). The federal Department of Industry, Trade and Commerce has underwritten a recently published investigation of Canada's renewable energy resources (Smith 1979). Original plans for a conserver society "test market" gradually evolved into a different kind of study -- now underway -- of whether community development techniques could serve as an important new ingredient in gaining widespread support for energy conservation programs formulated and implemented by an involved citizenry (Shapiro 1979).

OTHER IMPORTANT CANADIAN LITERATURE

Much of the literature most relevant to an investigation of the impact of Canada's Conserver Society studies has now been reviewed. However, a number of other Canadian publications might profitably be inspected by American marketers with a serious interest in the topic. Particular attention should be paid to the work of William Leiss, who raises some fundamental issues regarding needs, wants, commodities and "the good life." Leiss' monograph, <u>The Limits to Satisfaction</u>, completed by the end of 1975, contained a chapter on The Conserver Society (1976). Leiss also prepared a more detailed background paper on human needs for the Science Council's Conserver Society study (1975).

Certain of the studies sponsored by the Advanced Concepts Centre of the federal Department of the Environment, but especially McCallum's report on <u>Environmentally Appropriate Technology</u> (1977) and Starrs' <u>Canadians in Conversation About the Future</u> (1976), are well worth reading, as is Jackson's monograph, <u>Human Goals and Science Policy</u> (1976). A forthcoming paper discusses in some detail both the inevitability of a conserver society and the many different ways in which such a society will affect Canadian marketing management (Haines et al. 1980). Finally, the Energy Conservation Research Program now being conducted by Consumer and Corporate Affairs Canada should be of particular interest to marketing researchers, social marketers and, more generally, to any one concerned with the process of attitude change. However, that program is the subject of another submission to this publication.

THE REMAINING UNCERTAINTY:
THE IMPACT ON LIFE STYLES

In closing, attention must also be called to a vital area of investigation that, to date, has been inadequately explored. Whether Canadian consumers are prepared to substitute a conserver ethos for a long-standing and deep-seated commitment to mass consumption remains to be determined. The well publicized Stanford Research Institute study of "Voluntary Simplicity" has been embraced by most Canadian proponents of the Conserver Society (Elgin and Mitchell 1977). However, no literature presently exists on the attitudes currently held by Canadians along the many dimensions of the conserver-consumer spectrum. Unfortunately, a major survey of consumer perceptions of The Quality of Canadian Life, conducted during the Spring of 1979, failed to explore this topic in any real depth.

This absence of hard data notwithstanding, qualitative indications of an increased Canadian willingness to adopt a conserver ethos are to be found. Research now being conducted under the auspices of the Vanier Institute of the Family suggests a modest degree of movement toward conserver-consistent life styles in other areas besides energy. The National Survival Institute has been especially active in generating "grass roots" support for the conserver society concept and in facilitating adoption of conserver-consistent behaviour. A number of other groups all across Canada are involved in the areas of recycling, soft energy and appropriate technology.

The most significant initiative, perhaps, is that of Sudbury 2001 -- no splinter group of "would be reformers" but a multi-party, self-help effort with a leadership drawn from labour, business, government, academic and other key interest areas. Sudbury 2001 is the official economic development agency in a sizeable (170,000) Northern Ontario mining community. However, it is an organization which advocates Sudbury's becoming a conserver society and which links economic development with such conserver society components as appropriate scale and technology, ecological balance, decentralization and increased opportunities for personal creativity.

LOOKING BACKWARD -- AND AHEAD

This review of the intellectual and social impact of Canada's two conserver society studies is now complete. Research, writing, discussion and debate -- these have been the dominant activities of the last five years. The impact of the conserver society and its proponents on consumer behaviour, corporate practice and public policy has been a limited one. Indications exist, however, that the conserver option is beginning to make progress at the expense of the prevailing Canadian commitment to affluence, growth and mass consumption. The likely long term effects and, of course, the extent to which conserver society research will have contributed to such effects remains to be determined. To some of us, however, the direction in which all industrialized societies must move is already clear. Marketing, whether viewed primarily as academic discipline, societal function or corporate activity, can not help but be revolutionized in a world that -- willingly or unwillingly -- both values and legislates in favour of resource conservation, less materialistic life styles and ecologically responsible corporate marketing.

REFERENCES

Elgin, Duane S. and Arnold Mitchell (1977), "Voluntary Simplicity: Life Style of the Future?" The Futurist, (August), 200-209, 254-261.

Haines, George, Jr., George J. Leonidas and Monty Sommers (1980), "Impacts of the Conserver Society on Canadian Marketing Management," in Macromarketing: A Canadian Perspective, Donald Thompson et al., eds., Chicago: American Marketing Association.

Henion, Karl E. and Thomas C. Kinnear, eds. (1976), Ecological Marketing, Chicago: American Marketing Association.

Jackson, R.W. (1976), Background Study No. 38: Human Goals and Science Policy, Ottawa: Ministry of Supply and Services.

Leiss, William (1976), The Limits to Satisfaction: An essay on the problem of needs and commodities, Toronto: University of Toronto Press.

_____ (1975), "The Problem of Human Needs in the Consumer Society," A paper prepared for the Science Council of Canada, Ottawa Science Council.

McCallum, Bruce (1977), Renewable Energy and Other Developing Technologies for a Conserver Society in Canada, 4th edition, Ottawa: Department of Supply and Services.

Ministry of State for Science and Technology (1979), The Conserver Society: The Technological Challenge, Background Papers, Ottawa: MOSST.

Molitar, Graham T. (1977), "The Hatching of Public Opinion," Planning Review, (July), 3-7.

Science Council of Canada (1976a), Conserver Society Notes, (May-June), 2.

_____ (1976b), Statement of Concern, (February).

_____ (1977), Report No. 27 - Canada as a Conserver Society: Resource Uncertainties and the Need for New Technologies, Ottawa: Department of Supply and Services.

Science Forum (1976), 9, Numbers 3, 5, and 6.

Shapiro, Stanley J. (1979), "A New Approach to Ecologically Responsible Consumption: Community Involvement in Energy," in Macro-Marketing: New Steps on the Learning Curve, G. Fisk and R.W. Nason, eds., Boulder: Business Research Division, University of Colorado.

_____ (1976), "The Marketing System and the Conserver Society," Study No. 7, Vol. III in The Institutional Dimension, J.G. Smith, ed., Montreal: GAMMA.

Smith, J.G. (1979), "The Renewable Energy Business Sector in Canada: Structure, Performance and Prospects," Journal of Business Administration (Fall/Spring).

Starrs, Cathy (1976), Canadians in Conversation about the Future - Report No. 12, Ottawa: Office of the Science Advisor, Department of Fisheries and Environment.

Valaskakis, Kimon, Peter S. Sindell and J. Graham Smith (1977a), The Selective Conserver Society, Montreal: GAMMA.

_____, _____, _____, Iris Fitzpatrick-Martin (1979), The Conserver Society: A Workable Alternative for the Future, New York: Harper & Row.

_____, J.G. Smith, Peter S. Sindell and I. Martin (1977b), "The Conserver Society," Planning Review, (September), 16-22.

_____, (1979), The Information Society: The Issue and the Choices, Montreal: GAMMA.

PART TWO

THE CONSERVER

   This part delimits the characteristics and personality traits of consumers in the Conserver Society; also measures and describes the behavior and attitudes of consumers toward energy conservation and other socially responsible consumption.

THE CONSERVER SOCIETY? CONSUMERS' ATTITUDES AND BEHAVIORS REGARDING ENERGY CONSERVATION[1]

Jeffrey S. Milstein
Office of Conservation and Solar Applications
U.S. Department of Energy[2]

INTRODUCTION

In 1979, energy consumers have again faced gasoline lines and steeply rising electricity, heating fuel, and gasoline prices. The Iranian revolution has resulted in a reduction of oil from that country and tightened world oil markets. Controlling the amount of oil produced to keep the markets tight, the Organization of Petroleum Exporting Countries (OPEC) has significantly increased the price of oil during 1979. This has exacerbated the negative balance of trade of the United States, weakened the dollar, and added to inflation for American consumers. These adverse economic consequences of using imported oil are a major reason why the U.S. Government has tried to promote energy conservation over the past six years. An additional reason for reducing the U.S. dependence on foreign oil is to reduce the potential influence OPEC countries have on the domestic and foreign policies of the United States. History has shown twice in five years that foreign oil is not all that dependable.

ATTITUDES TOWARDS THE ENERGY SITUATION

It is important to understand some basic underlying attitudes of American consumers towards the energy situation and

---

[1] This paper draws on information from many surveys conducted since 1973 for the Federal Energy Administration and the Department of Energy, as well as many other more commonly reported surveys. Readers desiring more detailed information may contact me at the U.S. Department of Energy, Office of Conservation and Solar Applications, Washington, DC 20585.

[2] The findings and interpretations in this document do not necessarily represent the official policies, either expressed or implied, of the U.S. Department of Energy or of the U.S. Government.

their own use of energy in order to be able to design an effective approach to promoting energy conservation in America. Three generic attitudes of great importance include <u>cynicism</u>, <u>materialism</u>, and <u>faith in technology</u>.

<u>Cynicism</u>

Since the time of the Arab oil embargo of 1973-74, a significant fraction of Americans has held a cynical or skeptical attitude towards the energy situation. More than one-half of the population feels that the energy situation has been and remains a hoax perpetrated by the oil companies (and/or the OPEC countries) to increase their prices and profits. Others feel it is a situation caused or manipulated by politicians for their own purposes. Twice as many define the situation in this way as define it either as a real supply shortage or as a result of consumers using too much energy.

This attitude always has been a barrier to people's practicing energy conservation; people do not like being manipulated for the gain of others. Moreover, people saw that, after the 1973-74 Arab oil embargo and price rises, supplies were once again abundant. They therefore reasoned that the shortage was manipulated in order to obtain the price increases. That model tended to be the one commonly adopted during the supply shortfalls of 1979. In addition, when people did conserve electricity during the 1973-74 embargo, many utilities raised their unit rates in order to meet their income objectives. This reinforced many people's attitudes that conservation did not pay.

As a consequence, only about half of the American public thinks the national energy problem is, or will be, very serious. People have been concerned and aroused about the energy situation, mainly, if it affects them directly, immediately and perceivably. When people have to line up and wait to get gasoline; when their energy bills go up much faster than the general rate of inflation; when factories close down and people are out of work because of a natural gas shortage—<u>then</u> people are more concerned about the energy problem, because then it is their <u>own</u> problem. Then it is not just some abstract national or international problem that they have no control over, and which they feel has to be left to the "experts" to deal with (whether they are political leaders or technicians).

<u>Materialism</u>

Americans live in a fairly affluent society and place a high value on satisfying their comforts and conveniences. Ownership and consumption of material goods has a high value in the American culture. High status is given, for example, to the person who owns a large house and drives a big, expensive car.

People in our culture work in order to become successful, and energy-consuming material goods and activities are an important way in which people signal their success. Since the energy shortage of 1973, people have only reluctantly given up comforts or conveniences. Fuel economy is much less important to people in their choice of a car than is comfort or performance. The car is a convenience people depend on for mobility and tying together parts of their lives that are located in various places in and around large metropolitan areas. Labor-saving devices that consume energy in their manufacture and use abound in people's daily lives. People are reluctant to be too cool in the winter or too warm in the summer, since energy devices like air conditioners and furnaces can provide any level of comfort people desire.

These values, attitudes, and cultural norms have existed since well before the energy situation became a problem for most Americans. These values do, however, affect people's desire for and use of energy, and must be taken into account in designing any effort to promote energy conservation in America.

The materialistic American dream, while a major current in American values, is neither universal nor unmixed. Over the past generation, a large majority of Americans have established a satisfactory level of material well-being. Additional material goods are now giving people relatively less marginal satisfaction. As a consequence, people have increasingly had the desire to enjoy more of the intangibles of life, have more varied experiences, and develop themselves physically, intellectually, emotionally, socially, and spiritually. People are eating out more, traveling more, becoming physically fit by jogging and playing tennis, reading more books, being more involved in developing their interpersonal relationships, and developing their spiritual selves.

Changing values and patterns of life have different effects on energy consumption. Two-thirds of all the energy used in America goes to personal consumption: one-third directly for propelling cars, heating homes, running appliances, etc.; and one-third for the manufacture, transportation, processing, etc., of the goods consumers use. One of the ways people have attempted to cope with chronic inflation is to try to make these consumer goods last longer. This is one of the reasons for changing consumer spending habits. To the extent that consumers use their incomes to buy fewer goods, energy demands are reduced. On the other hand, to the extent that people travel more, fuel demands shift for different kinds of energy (e.g., more gasoline and jet fuel, possibly less coal in manufacturing). Other new lifestyles and values increase the demand for energy. For example, half of all women between the ages of 21 and 49 are now employed outside the home. Working women demand more time-saving devices for the household and a second car to get to and from their jobs.

The main concern consumers have about energy has been the price they have to pay, except when energy availability itself is in question. People do not want to pay higher prices or taxes for the energy they use, nor do they want to give up their comforts, conveniences, or lifestyles that energy makes possible. The rising price of energy is the energy problem to a majority of people. Oil companies and oil producing countries are perceived as the cause of the price rises, enriching themselves at the expense of the consumer. The price of energy is what the consumer experiences weekly and monthly when paying for his gasoline or utilities. Thus they are of much greater salience than more distant or abstract notions like national dependence, balance of trade, or various macro-economic concepts like supply and demand. Thus, consumers often do not understand the proposal to solve our national energy problem by raising their energy prices. "How can you solve high prices by making them even higher?", they ask.

Consumer concern about the price of energy, however, is the most important motivator for energy conservation for a majority of consumers. Fewer are motivated by a concern about dwindling resources or such altruistic reasons as citizen responsibility. This motivation reflects the underlying materialistic values held by Americans. People tend to be selfish, and thus feel strongly that any sacrifice, such as cutting back their energy use or paying more for energy, be equitably shared. This applies to all classes of consumers, as well as to business and government. People do not even want to go 55 miles per hour on the highway if others pass them. They certainly do not want to make more financial, mobility, or material sacrifices than anyone else, including the oil companies.

Faith in Technology
Another widely held belief in America is that there are technological solutions to problems, including the Nation's energy problem. Since technology is felt to be the domain of "experts," this faith in technology removes from consumers the perceived need to handle the problem with their own hands. "If America can devleop the atomic bomb and put a man on the moon, it surely can solve its energy problem," is a popularly stated belief. Many people feel that new sources of energy, such as solar energy, or liquid fuels derived from coal or shale, or (until the Three Mile Island accident) nuclear power, will save them from the need to really change their lifestyles in order to use less energy. A vast majority of people support the government in its effort to do research and develop new energy

sources. This belief in an almost magical technological solution that will somehow save them removes from people the perceived need to take personal actions to conserve energy to help cope with the problem. A technological "holy grail" relieves people from seeing that the "Kingdom of Heaven" is within; i.e., to look to themselves for solutions to their own problems. This belief in technology, it should be noted, is reinforced by many of the messages which the government and industry send to the public. Every new technological advance is highly publicized, but less well publicized is how long the technology will take to develop and produce on a large-scale basis.

AWARENESS OF THE ENERGY SITUATION AND HOW TO SAVE ENERGY

An important characteristic of a large fraction of American consumers is a <u>lack of knowledge</u> about the nature of the energy situation and what they as individuals can <u>specifically</u> do about it. Half of all Americans do not even know that the country must import oil to meet its own needs. Only about one quarter of the people know how much oil the U.S. imports. Only half of young adults answered correctly fifty key energy questions in a national survey by the National Assessment of Educational Progress (1978). Four-tenths of the people do not know their water heater temperature setting. Four in ten do not realize that lowering their home's temperatures one or two degrees saves energy. Half the drivers who drive alone in their cars to work do not think this wastes energy. Only one-third of consumers can cite specific practices by individuals or households that can save energy.

This lack of information points to a continuing need to inform consumers more specifically about the nature of the energy situation we face, and especially what, specifically, consumers can do to cope with their own situations. Without such informed awareness, it is difficult to establish the attitudes that are favorable towards energy conservation and to get consumers to practice energy conservation. The less informed people are, the less receptive they are to appeals for energy conservation.

CONSERVATION BEHAVIORS

In spite of the lack of much important information, and of cynical and materialistic attitudes, Americans have conserved energy in many important ways. The behavioral pattern is spotty, however. Partly because they do believe in technical solutions to problems, Americans have tended to perform those energy conserving behaviors which make their homes or cars more technically fuel-<u>efficient</u>. Thus, more than four out of five households now have some insulation. (That is not the same as saying they are adequately insulated according to recommended standards.) Half of American homeowners have added insulation to their homes over the past five years, at about the rate of one-tenth of homeowners per year. About seven in ten homes have storm windows or storm doors, and the sales of these energy-conserving items have been rising every year, with about one in ten homeowners purchasing some. Since insulation or adding storm windows to homes are very important energy conservation practices, this is perhaps the best example of the successful promotion of voluntary energy conservation in America.

Another example of American consumers' practicing energy conservation is in their purchase of more fuel-efficient cars. In 1979, seven in ten new cars sold were "small" cars. In this case, consumer purchasing decisions have been influenced by the legal requirement that auto manufacturers must meet fleet average gasoline mileage standards each year. The 1978 new car fleet averaged forty-one percent greater fuel efficiency than the 1974 new car fleet, according to Environmental Protection Agency tests. Since purchasing a more fuel-efficient car is the single most important energy conservation practice in the personal transportation area, this is a very significant accomplishment.

Note that the purchase of insulation or a more efficient car is usually a one-time behavior on the part of consumers. Energy-conserving behaviors which must be maintained over time, especially those that require sacrifice of comfort or convenience, are less well practiced.

Half the people do turn out lights that are not needed. Moreover, the average indoor summertime temperature in homes with operating air conditioners is 80 degrees (as measured with thermometers)--the recommended temperature. However, the average measured indoor temperature in winter is 70 degrees, five degrees above the recommended level. Only about four-tenths of households lower their thermostats at night in winter, with the average nighttime temperature in winter being 69 degrees.

In the area of personal transportation, two-thirds of Americans drive alone to and from work in urban areas. About one in five shares a ride, and that proportion actually declined from 1972 (when one-quarter shared rides) to 1978. Only one in eight people regularly rides urban public transit to and from work. One in twenty walks to and from work. The convenience of solo driving is not given up easily by American consumers.

Highway speeds, which averaged 60 miles per hour in 1973, declined to 55 mph in 1974 after the new speed limit took effect. But after the embargo, they rose steadily again, although not all the way up to their previous high average.

Half of all American households take a vacation trip by car every year, with the average number being more than two trips per year by these vacationing households. The average travel party consists of three people, typically a family. The average mileage driven per year is about 3,500 for all household vacations. This is about 30 percent of all miles driven per year by these households.

Vacation trips by car took a temporary dip during the spring of 1974 (during the oil embargo) and during the 1975 recession following the embargo. Starting with the 1976 Bicentennial year, vacation travel has since steadily increased. While it is too early at this writing to determine the effect of the 1979 gasoline shortage on vacation travel (except to note that the railroads are booked solid), between gasoline shortages Americans used a large amount of gasoline on their vacation travel--an integral part of the lifestyles of a majority of Americans.

Thus, the promotion of energy conservation behavior has had a mixed success since the Arab oil embargo of 1973-74. It seems clear that it is easier to obtain conservation through one-time product purchase behavior than it is to sustain a behavior over time, especially one that involves a complex social behavior such as ridesharing.

PROMOTING ENERGY CONSERVATION

Americans get most of their information about energy (indeed, about most things outside their personal experience) from the mass media--particularly television and newspapers. In order to promote energy conservation effectively, these must be the primary channels used for communication.

The information communicated must also come from a credible source. Surveys have shown that source credibility has two major dimensions--the source must be considered "expert," i.e., one must have reason to know that what the "expert" is saying is correct; and the source must be seen as having no vested economic or political interest in energy. Thus, university scientists and fellow consumers who have had some personal experience with some energy conservation practice are more credible than government or industry representatives. The media are themselves also a credible source of information on energy to consumers. In addition, friends who have had personal experience are also credible to consumers. A strategy to promote energy conservation must thus use the mass media and rely on the multi-step ripple effect of communications among consumers.

Energy conservation can be effectively promoted if it is shown as being rewarding to the consumers practicing it, especially if information can be fed back to them about the rewarding effect. Consumers do not want to sacrifice, but energy conservation can be positioned as personally rewarding.

CONCLUSION

To promote energy conservation effectively, we must understand where consumers are _now_; what they know and do not know; what their feelings and attitudes about energy issues are; and what they already have or have not done.

There is still a great need for energy conservation in this country, as well as a need to clearly communicate to the energy consumers of this country the continuing nature of our country's energy situation, including its international context; what consumers can do about their own energy situation; and the progress that has been made so far.

After six years, we may feel that we have been through this effort to promote conservation before; but given the continuing situation, this effort must continue.

REFERENCE

National Assessment of Education Progress (1978), _Energy: Knowledge and Attitudes._ Prepared for the National Center for Education Statistics, U.S. Department of Health, Education, and Welfare (December)

CONSTRUCTION AND VALIDATION OF A SCALE
TO MEASURE SOCIALLY RESPONSIBLE
CONSUMPTION BEHAVIOR[1]

John H. Antil, University of Vermont
Peter D. Bennett, The Pennsylvania State University

INTRODUCTION

In recent years, the deterioration of our environment and the awareness of the severity of the depletion of our natural resources have prompted considerable interest in more responsible production and consumption as means for controlling our environmental and resource-related problems. Consumer behavior researchers have focused on determining and more fully understanding the characteristics of the socially environmentally responsible consumer (c.f. Anderson and Cunningham 1972; Brooker 1976, Henion 1972, 1976; Herberger 1975; Kassarjian 1971; Kinnear and Taylor 1973; Kinnear, Taylor and Ahmed 1974; Maloney, Ward and Braucht 1975; Mayer 1976; Murphy, Kangun and Locander 1978; Tognacci et al. 1972; Webster 1975).

Socially responsible consumption and other terms which are used in a conceptually similar manner have been frequently found in the literature. Yet there does not appear to be much consistency in the various terminologies and definitions that have been offered. Examples are "responsible consumption" (Fisk 1973); "socially conscious consumer" (Anderson and Cunningham 1972; Webster 1975); "societal economics" (Herberger 1975); "ecologically concerned consumer" (Henion 1976). Nevertheless, each appears to be concerned with what is apparently a similar individual difference construct.

In the present research a definition similar to that proposed by Henion (1976) has been developed. Socially responsible consumption is defined as those consumer behaviors and purchase decisions which are related to environmental and resource-related problems and are motivated not only by a desire to satisfy personal needs, but also by a concern for the welfare of society in general.

---

[1]The authors express their appreciations to the Center for the Study of Environmental policy of The Pennsylvania State University and to the American Marketing Association for the financial and other assistance which made this research possible. Those readers interested in a more detailed discussion refer to Antil (1978) or Antil and Bennett (1979).

There appear to be many degrees of consumption behavior that is socially responsible. These range from purchase behavior which shows little concern beyond the immediate satisfaction of the buyers' personal needs to that which exhibits considerable concern for any effects such behavior has on the buyers' environment and on society in general. Thus, socially responsible consumption is not a behavioral pattern which a consumer either has or does not have. Rather it is a behavioral pattern that is exhibited in varying degrees.

Perhaps the most serious problem in the study of consumption that is socially and environmentally responsible has been the use by investigators of varying methodologies to identify the socially responsible consumer. These have ranged from classifying a consumer as socially responsible if he/she reports purchasing one or more environmentally compatible products (e.g., lead-free gasoline, phosphate-free detergents) to using a variety of attitudinal scales. Hence, it is unsurprising that the results of these investigations have provided conflicting evidence regarding the characteristics of this consumer type. Though dependent variables used by investigators are intended to be similar, in none of their studies do they report evidence that consumers have been isolated according to a conceptually similar dimension.

What is needed is a reliable and valid measure that is relatively easy to administer, is consumption-related, and is able to classify consumers according to their degree of socially responsible consumption. The Socially Responsible Consumption Behavior Scale (SRCB Scale) presented here is intended to fill this void in consumer behavior research.

SCALE CONSTRUCTION METHODOLOGY

Although this research preceded the procedure suggested by Churchill (1979), the methods employed in the development of the SRCB Scale closely parallel those suggested by that researcher.

To assure that the SRCB Scale was both reliable and valid several steps were taken. These included: (1) extensive pretesting on relatively large samples, (2) item analysis and factor analysis performed during several phases of the development of the scale, (3) validation using the "known groups" technique and a reduced version of Campbell and Fiske's (1970) multitrait-multimethod procedure for construct validation, and (4) administration and test of the final scale on a national sample of households.

Item Selection for First Pretest

The initial pool of items consisted of 138 positively and negatively worded statements. Some items considered to be conceptually related to the construct of socially responsible consumption behavior were selected from existing scales (Tognacci, et al. 1972; Maloney, Ward and Braucht 1975; Nelson 1974; Kinnear and Taylor 1973). Other items were developed after reviewing the literature on the relationship between consumption and environmental or resource-related problems. Of the original 138 items, 14 were eliminated because they were redundant, ambiguous, or did not appear to be clearly positive or negative statements. The remaining 124 items (using a five-point Likert-type scale) were divided into two relatively equivalent scales, one consisting of 63 items (Form A) and the other containing 61 (Form B). This division was necessary in order to reduce the time necessary to complete the questionnaire. Next, these two forms were pretested on a convenience sample of 444 students at Penn State University. They represented a somewhat diversified cross section consisting of undergraduate and graduate students from 18 different classes.

The results of the pretest were then submitted to both a factor analysis and an item analysis. Each statistical technique contributes in different ways toward the same common goal: an attitude scale that has acceptable levels of reliability and validity. Factor analysis can be used to identify those items which are highly correlated with one another on any single dimension and also to divide the data into a number of orthogonal (or oblique) factors or dimensions. Thus, the investigator can be more certain of what underlying dimension(s) his scale is actually measuring. One problem with factor analysis is that it is often difficult to identify and interpret factors. Another problem is that the investigator has considerable latitude as to how the data are to be manipulated and what assumptions are to be made. Such problems can result in a variety of interpretations of the same data.

Compared with factor analysis, item analysis is rather straightforward. Its purpose is to obtain internal consistency, thereby increasing the reliability of the scale. Its key calculation is the adjusted item-to-total correlation (hereafter called item-total correlation), which is the correlation between the score on a single item and the score on the total scale (with the item of concern removed). By selecting only those statements with reasonably strong item-total correlations, the internal consistency of the scale should be acceptable and the investigator can be more confident that the items in his scale are all measuring the same trait(s). Further, an item analysis offers some indication of an item's ability to discriminate between respondents with favorable and unfavorable attitudes. This is accomplished through the use of a t statistic, which is derived from a comparison between extreme groups of mean responses on an attitudinal item (e.g., the highest 27 percent compared to the lowest 27 percent of respondents). Though this is not a powerful test, it is useful as a guide and is especially helpful in eliminating items which have little discriminating ability.

Normally, item analysis is used for item reduction and factor analysis to determine the number of dimensions represented in the final scale. In this research, however, an attempt was made to use simultaneously both analytical methods to eliminate items from an item pool. For this purpose item analysis was much more useful, although in general the results from both methods were similar. Factor analysis was helpful during the final stage of the development of the scale when the aim was to eliminate any items that were so highly intercorrelated that they were measuring essentially the same thing. (Such a condition if present was revealed in the inter-item correlation matrix). However, the principal purpose of factor analysis was to identify various dimensions in the data collected at different stages. Only the results for the final stage are reported.

The initial item reduction was accomplished by excluding those items which had an item-total correlation less than .4 and a factor loading less than .4 on any factor (using principal factor analysis with iterations and communality estimates in the main diagonal). Both forms of the scale showed high indices of reliability in their unreduced form (coefficient alpha index of reliability was .928 for Form A and .915 for Form B). Combined, the scales contained 75 items with item-total correlations greater than .4 and 25 **items** greater than .5.

This procedure resulted in the elimination of 19 items from Form A and 21 items from Form B. At this early stage it was decided to retain all items with factor loadings greater than .4 even if their item-total correlations were below the established cut-off of .4. This was done in order to see if the items with "high" factor loadings and low item-total correlations would improve reliability in the next stage of analysis when the number of items would be considerably reduced. This was not found to be the case; a low item-total correlation was nearly always accompanied by a relatively low factor loading. The elimination of these 40 items resulted in only a slight reduction in the reliability of each form (coefficient alpha was .923 for Form A and .911 for Form B).

The procedure established for the second set of item eliminations differed from the first in that the item-total correlation was the sole criterion used to select items for omission. Initially, a .4 item-total correlation was again used as a minimum level of acceptability. However, in order to reduce the number of items on both forms to a level which approached the objective number of items (30 on each form), the .4 cut-off had to be increased for Form A since it contained too few items below that figure. (In retrospect, establishing a higher item-total correlation for one form over the other was less important than simply eliminating those items with the lowest item-total correlations, regardless of whether they were on Forms A or B). Accordingly, 12 items were omitted from Form A and 8 from Form B, leaving 32 items for each form or 64 in all. Again, these reductions did not significantly affect the reliability of either form (Form A's α decreased from .923 to .912, while Form B's remained the same, .911).

The last set of items to be dropped from the scale was determined by considering item-total correlations and factor loadings. Any item with an item-total correlation less than .4 was eliminated, as was any item which did not have its highest factor loading on the first factor. Four items failed to meet the first requirement and one, the second requirement. With the elimination of these five items, a total of 59 items remained after the pretest. (Since only one item, instead of several, was removed from the scale because its highest factor loading was not on the first factor, there was little risk of forcing the scale to become unidimensional).

Item Selection for Second Pretest

The 59 items remaining after the first pretest were combined into one questionnaire and administered to undergraduates in an introductory marketing course. Questionnaires were received from 382 students; 321 questionnaires were sufficiently complete to be used for analysis.

The first step was to eliminate eight items whose item-total correlations were less than .3. Their correlations ranged from .207 to .297.

Next, 13 of the remaining items whose item-total correlations were still less than .4 were examined for possible elimination in order to reduce the scale at this stage to 40 to 45 items. Eight items were eliminated because either they were not directly related to products and consumption behavior or they also had shown low correlations in the first pretest. The former criterion for elimination received the greater weight.

The final step in the selection of items was to review the inter-item correlation matrix for the remaining 43 items in order to identify any pair whose items were highly intercorrelated. Only one pair was so identified (r=.7) and on examination the items were found to have little conceptual difference and hence were probably measuring the same thing. The item in the pair with the lower item-total correlation was eliminated.

Even after reducing the 59 items by 17 items, the remaining 42 items comprised a scale whose reliability was almost exactly the same as the longer one (coefficient alphas of .923 vs. .929, respectively). The number of items on the shorter scale was not unwarrantly large for a respondent to handle. Yet it was large enough so that some items could still be eliminated in the final pretest and still leave enough items comprising a final scale with acceptable reliability.

Adult Pretest

The 42-item SRCB Scale was once again pretested on a group of 98 male and female non-student adults. This sample consisted of members of a civic organization and a church group from Northampton, Massachusetts, and parents from two elementary school cooperatives in Burlington, Vermont. The organizations were paid $3.00 for each completed questionnaire received. This pretest differed from the previous two in that the scale was only one section of a much larger 26-page research instrument. The results from the final pretest indicated the SRCB Scale performed very well on this sample of adults. Reliability was again high (.942). Two items whose item-total correlations were less than .3 were eliminated, leaving a scale of 40 items to be incorporated in the final research instrument (Appendix).

DATA COLLECTION FOR NATIONAL SAMPLE

In June 1977, a twelve-page research instrument (containing the SRCB Scale) was mailed to 1,000 households who were members of a consumer mail panel maintained by Market Facts, Inc. The sample of 500 males and 500 females was selected from the over 65,000 households retained by Market Facts for use in mail surveys. The national sample of households was balanced according to the latest census data on four demographic variables: geographic region, annual household income, population density and degree of urbanization, and age of panel member. Useable questionnaires were returned by 736 respondents, or about 74 percent of the total sample. In a comparison of respondents and nonrespondents on the questionnaire, it was determined that no differences existed along the demographic dimensions which would significantly affect the analysis of results. No follow-up of non-respondents was attempted.

In addition to the national sample, the SRCB Scale and one additional question also were mailed to a sample of 150 members of the New England Chapter of the Sierra Club. Eighty-five Sierra Club members returned questionnaires suitable for analysis.

Statistical Analysis

The range of scores for the SRCB Scale was from a low of 64 to a high of 200. The mean score was 144.5, which was also very close to the median of 145. Further, 48.1 percent of the total received scores of 143 or less, while 50.3 percent had scores of 145 or greater. The standard deviation was 24.3, and the variance was 589.9. The figure for skewness was -.295 and for kurtosis it was -.005. **See Table 1 for score distribution.**

Reliability

The SRCB Scale was found to have excellent reliability based on two different measures. The indexes of reliability for Guttman's Lamda 3 and for Cronbach's coefficient alpha were .930 and .925, respectively.

Dimensionality

Results of factor analysis of pretest data indicated that the SRCB Scale was unidimensional. Consequently, the initial step in looking for the dimensionality of the final 40-item scale given to the national sample was to obtain a five-factor solution. As had been previously used (along with other variations) principal factor analysis with iterations to improve communality estimates was employed. Table 2 presents the results of this analysis. The large drop in the magnitude of the eigenvalues and the percent of explained variance after the first factor presents fairly strong evidence that the scale items appeared to be measuring a predominantly unidimensional construct. An examination of the varimax rotated factors did not appear to demonstrate any significant difference in the conceptual meaning of the items within each of the five factors.

TABLE 1
FREQUENCY OF SRCB SCALE SCORES

Score	Frequency	Score	Frequency
<70	2	131-140	107
71-80	7	141-150	105
81-90	8	151-160	105
91-100	13	161-170	83
101-110	28	171-180	59
111-120	45	181-190	26
121-130	88	191-200	14

TABLE 2

RESULTS OF PRINCIPAL FACTOR ANALYSIS ON
SRCB SCALE USING NATIONAL SAMPLE

Five-Factor Solution

Factor	Eigenvalue	Explained variance (%)
1	9.96	69.4
2	1.56	10.8
3	1.25	8.7
4	.95	6.6
5	.64	4.4

Three-Factor Solution

1	9.91	78.3
2	1.53	12.1
3	1.21	9.6

Although the results appear to substantiate the same conclusions as were reached in the pretest phase of the development of the SRCB Scale, a three-factor solution was also performed to further verify the number of apparently significant factors. Once again, as Table 2 clearly indicates, the first factor almost completely dominated the remaining two factors. An examination of the factor matrix revealed only three items with their highest factor loadings on the second or third factors.

Scale Validation

This scale was first examined for face validity. The examination was based on a conceptual review of item content and it was clear that the SRCB Scale passed this elementary test extremely well.

Kerlinger and Kaya (1970) have suggested that the logical validity of a scaling device can be measured through factor analysis. This form of validity requires that the individual items comprising the scale are all related to one or more recognizable and definable dimensions. The factor analytic

procedures followed in this research showed strong evidence
that the SRCB Scale was primarily measuring a single dimension.
Consequently, the SRCB Scale has logical validity.

A commonly used validation technique is the "known groups"
method (Kerlinger and Kaya 1970). This procedure **requires**
the administration of a scale to a group believed to possess a
considerable amount of the trait under consideration and a
comparison of these results with those obtained from a random
group, or where available, a sample known to have a small
amount of the trait. In the present case, the mean SRCB Scale
scores from the national sample (n=690) and Sierra Club sample
(n=85) were compared and significant differences ($p<.01$) were
found between the respective means of 144.3 versus 168.5. Such
a finding lends considerable support to the predictive validity
of the present scale (Kerlinger and Kaya 1970).

In an effort to further establish the validity of the SRCB
Scale, a variation (reduced form) of Campbell and Fiske's (1970)
multitrait-multimethod for construct validation was employed.
In essence this method requires using at lease two different
methods of measurement (e.g., summated rating scale, semantic
differential) and at least two different traits. Campbell and
Fiske do not specify how the traits should be selected. However, it appears that they should be conceptually related to
each other, but not be so similar that they measure the same
underlying trait. In their suggested procedure, correlations
obtained between the various trait-method combinations are
compared.

In the present study, it was not possible to follow
strictly the procedure outlined by Campbell and Fiske. Few
other scales are presently available which were designed to
measure traits related to the present construct. Consequently,
these scales would have to be developed, a task which would
require an excessive amount of time and expense. However, it
was possible to adopt some of the same techniques recommended
to establish the validity of the scale.

The present study utilized three traits: traditional
social responsibility, ecological concern, and the socially
responsible consumption behavior construct. Each of these
traits was measured using the Likert method. The scale
developed by Berkowitz and Daniels (1964)--and further tested
and reduced by Berkowitz and Lutterman (1968)--and used in a
marketing context by Anderson and Cunningham (1972) to identify
the socially conscious consumer was utilized as the Likert-type
method to measure traditional social responsibility. As
reported by Anderson and Cunningham (1972, p. 25), this eight-
item scale is designed to "measure an individual's traditional

social responsibility, i.e., the willingness of an individual to help other persons even when there is nothing to be gained for himself."

Ecological concern was measured by a Likert-type scale developed by Maloney, Ward and Braucht (1975). Even though six of the items from the ten-item affect subscale were also included in the SRCB Scale, this scale was used due to the lack of other available scales to measure traits related to socially responsible consumption. However, such a scale is more likely to be highly correlated with the SRCB Scale than another similar scale without items common to both scales. Thus, there is a risk of getting a correlation so high that it appears that both the SRCB Scale and the ecological concern scale are measuring the same trait.

The SRCB Scale utilized the Likert method for measuring socially responsible consumption. In addition, this trait was also measured using a second and third method. For the second method a self-designation procedure was developed in which each respondent rated him/herself (and the average American) on a thermometer-type scale ranging from 0 to 100. Hypothetical individuals at the extremes of the scale were described as a guide to respondents in selecting their scores.

The third method used to operationalize the socially responsible consumption behavior construct was a self-reported behavioral measure (Behavior Index). A group of 34 diverse behaviors was selected based on the belief that they were the type of behaviors one would expect from the socially responsible consumer. The behaviors included in the Behavior Index were selected from a larger list of behaviors that were evaluated according to this basis by sixteen judges (marketing faculty and Ph.D. students at The Pennsylvania State University).

To reduce response bias and postpone awareness that questions were designed to measure behaviors that were related to the environment, 33 "dummy" behaviors were intermixed with the 34 selected behaviors. This disguised form of the Behavior Index was then placed in the first section of the research instrument.

Table 3 presents the multitrait-multimethod correlation matrix. The procedure employed in this study has retained enough of Campbell and Fiske's (1970) original concepts to maintain the intended integrity of their rigorous method of scale validation. The values labeled 1, 3, and 6 are not actual correlations, but are the reliability measures for each of these scales. No reliability figures were available for either the self-designated or the Behavior Index measure. The most useful correlations are those which measure the same trait by means of different methods (correlations 7, 10, and 13). In Campbell and Fisk's terminology these values would be considered components of the validity diagonal. The magnitudes of these correlations are compared to those of various other trait-method combinations.

TABLE 3

MULTITRAIT-MULTIMETHOD MATRIX
OF SCALE CORRELATIONS

Method		Likert			Self-designated
	Trait:	SRCB[1]	EC[2]	TSR[3]	SRCB
Likert	SRCB	1(.93)[a]			
	EC	2(.73)	3(.78)[a]		
	TSR	4(.29)	5(.17)	6(.55)[a]	
Self-designated	SRCB	7(.33)	8(.30)	9(.14)	
Behavior Index (Self-reported behavior)	SRCB	10(.56)	11(.45)	12(.25)	13(.35)

[1]SRCB = Socially Responsible Consumption Behavior
[2]EC = Ecological Concern
[3]TSR = Traditional Social Responsibility
[a]Coefficient alpha index of reliability

The first criterion suggested by Campbell and Fiske is that entries in the validity diagonal should be large enough to warrant further evaluation of validity. The aforementioned correlations are significantly different from zero ($p < .001$) and appear to be sufficiently large to encourage further examination of validity. The present correlations are evidence of convergent validity, namely that the scale correlates highly with other methods designed to measure the same construct.

Three additional criteria suggested by Campbell and Fiske provide evidence of discriminant validity or the degree to which a measure is unique and not a measure of another variable. Due to the lack of trait-method combinations available in the present research, only two of the three validation criteria were considered.

One of these requires a comparison of the validity values with correlations in the same row. The reason is that "a validity value for a variable should be higher than the correlations obtained between the variable and any other variable having neither trait nor method in common." (Campbell and Fiske, p. 101). This requirement is satisfied. The validity value of .33, correlation 7 of the SRCB trait by two different methods, is larger than correlations 8 (.30) and 9 (.14) which represent two different traits and two different methods. Likewise, validity value 10 (.56) is larger than correlations 11 (.45) and 12 (.25).

The other criterion for discriminant validity requires a comparison of validity values with those correlations derived from measuring different traits by the same method. The reason is that "a variable correlates higher with an independent effort to measure the same trait than with measures designed to get at different traits which happen to employ the same method" (Campbell and Fiske, p. 101). Referring to Table 2, this requires comparing the validity values, namely, correlations 7 and 10, with correlations 2, 4, and 5, respectively. Except for correlation 2 (.73), this requirement is satisfied. It is unsurprising that the correlation between the ecological concern scale and the SRCB Scale is so high. Conceptually, these two traits are highly related and the fact that six of the ten items included in the ecological concern scale were also included in the SRCB Scale clearly explains why this correlation is so high. As mentioned earlier this apparent disadvantage is sustainable owing to the shortage of scales for related traits.

In summary, there appears to be fairly strong evidence that the SRCB Scale exhibits an acceptable level of validity. The "known groups" method of evaluation and the results from the reduced version of Campbell and Fiske's multitrait-multimethod procedure for construct validation **indicate that the SRCB Scale does in fact measure the trait that it was designed to measure.**

DISCUSSION

For any scientific discipline to progress through the

cumulative efforts of many researchers, it is vital that their communications with each other be clear and unambiguous. Especially in the social sciences, we communicate in terms of constructs, but are rarely able to measure the constructs themselves, only aspects of them (Dubin 1969). It becomes extremely important, therefore, that the manner in which individual researchers operationalize their measurements of constructs be rigorous in terms of both reliability and validity.

It's equally important that different researchers operationalize the same construct in similar ways--or at least be fully aware of their differences--or their efforts are not likely to be cumulative, or even comparable. One indication of the maturity of a discipline, in fact, is just such consistency.

There is obviously no single best method to construct and validate measures of individual differences in marketing and consumer behavior. The need, however, for careful construction and validation exists and continued strides toward improved methods and procedures are of paramount importance to the advancement of marketing as a discipline.

This article has described a set of procedures used to construct and validate a measure of socially responsible consumption, a construct whose use in the literature has not been particularly consistent. The scale provided in the Appendix is available for use by future researchers who wish to pursue further the issue of socially responsible consumption. With its continued use and improvement, the discipline will have an even more useful empirical indicator of an individual difference variable of interest.

Also, this article has described the multiple procedures followed to evaluate the SRCB Scale for both reliability and validity. While these specific steps may not be appropriate for the evaluation of all other individual difference measures, they indicate a pattern which can lead to more dependable measures. They may appear tedious and time-consuming. They are. It is the price investigators must pay for improving the precision of the scientific language of marketing.

APPENDIX

TEST TO DETERMINE SOCIALLY RESPONSIBLE CONSUMPTION BEHAVIOR

People should be more concerned about reducing or limiting the noise in our society..

Every person should stop increasing their consumption of products so that our resources will last longer..............

The benefits of modern consumer products are more important than the pollution which results from their production and use...

Pollution is presently one of the most critical problems facing this nation..

I don't think we're doing enough to encourage manufacturers to use recyclable packages...

I think we are just not doing enough to save scarce natural resources from being used up.....................................

Natural resources must be preserved even if people must do without some products...

All consumers should be interested in the environmental consequences of the products they purchase.........................

Pollution is not personally affecting my life..................

Consumers should be made to pay higher prices for products which pollute the environment..

It genuinely infuriates me to think that the government doesn't do more to help control pollution of the environment..........

Nonreturnable bottles and cans for soft drinks and beer should be banned by law..

I would be willing to sign a petition or demonstrate for an environmental cause..

I have often thought that if we could just get by with a little less there would be more left for future generations..........

The Federal government should subsidize research on technology for recycling waste products.....................................

I'd be willing to ride a bicycle or take a bus to work in order to reduce air pollution..

I would probably never join a group or club which is concerned solely with ecological issues.................................

I feel people worry too much about pesticides on food products.

The whole pollution issue has never upset me too much since I feel it's somewhat overrated..................................

I would donate a day's pay to a foundation to help improve the environment......................................

I would be willing to have my laundry less white or bright in order to be sure that I was using a nonpolluting laundry product...

Manufacturers should be forced to use recycled materials in their manufacturing and processing operations................

I think that a person should urge her friends not to use products that pollute or harm the environment................

Commercial advertising should be forced to mention the ecological disadvantages of products...............................

Much more fuss is being made about air and water pollution than is really justified...

The government should provide each citizen with a list of agencies and organizations to which citizens could report grievances concerning pollution...........................

I would be willing to pay a 5 percent increase in my taxes to support greater governmental control of pollution.............

Trying to control water pollution is more trouble than it is worth..

I become incensed when I think about the harm being done to plant and animal life by pollution...........................

People should urge their friends to limit their use of products made from scarce resources....................................

I would be willing to pay one dollar more each month for electricity if it meant cleaner air..........................

It would be wise for the government to devote much more money toward supporting a strong conservation program...............

I would be willing to accept an increase in my family's total expenses of $120 next year to promote the wise use of natural resources..

Products which during their manufacturing or use pollute the environment should be heavily taxed by the government........

People should be willing to accept smog in exchange for the convenience of automobiles.................................

When I think of the ways industries are polluting I get frustrated and angry..

Our public schools should require all students to take a course dealing with environmental and conservation problems.........

I would be willing to stop buying products from companies guilty of polluting the environment even though it might be inconvenient...

I'd be willing to make personal sacrifices for the sake of slowing down pollution even though the immediate results may not seem significant.......................................

I rarely ever worry about the effects of smog on myself and family..

REFERENCES

Anderson, W. T. and W. Cunningham (1972), "The Socially Conscious Consumer," Journal of Marketing, 36 (July), 23-31.

Antil, J. (1978), "The Construction and Validation of an Instrument to Measure Socially Responsible Consumption," unpublished Doctoral Dissertation, Department of Marketing, The Pennsylvania State University.

Antil, J. and P. Bennett (1979), "The Construction and Validation of an Instrument to Measure Socially Responsible Consumption Behavior," Working Series in Energy-Environmental Policy, The Center for the Study of Environmental Policy, The Pennsylvania State University.

Berkowitz, L. and L. R. Daniels (1964), "Affecting the Salience of the Social Responsibility Norm: Effects of Past Help on the Response to Dependency Relationships," Journal of Abnormal and Social Psychology, 68 (March), 275-81.

_____, and K. G. Lutterman (1968), "The Traditional Socially Responsible Personality," Public Opinion Quarterly, 32 (Summer), 169-85.

Brooker, G. (1976), "The Self-Actualizing Socially Conscious Consumer," The Journal of Consumer Research, 3 (September), 107-12.

Campbell, D. T. and D. Fiske (1970), "Convergent and Discriminant Validation by the Multitrait-Multimethod Matrix," in <u>Attitude Measurement</u>, G. Summers, ed., Chicago: Rand McNally, 100-22.

Churchill, G. A. (1979), "A Paradigm for Developing Better Measures of Marketing Constructs," <u>Journal of Marketing Research</u>, 16 (February), 64-73.

Dubin, R. (1969), <u>Theory Building</u>. New York: The Free Press.

Fisk, G. (1973), "Criteria for a Theory of Responsible Consumption," <u>Journal of Marketing</u>, 37 (April), 24-31.

Henion, K. E. (1976), <u>Ecological Marketing</u>. Columbus: Grid Inc.

Henion, K. E. (1972), "The Effect of Ecologically Relevant Information on Detergent Sales," <u>Journal of Marketing Research</u>, 9 (February), 10-14.

Herberger, R. A., Jr. (1975), "The Ecological Product Buying Motive - A Challenge for Consumer Education," <u>The Journal of Consumer Affairs</u>, 9 (Winter), 187-95.

Kassarjian, H. (1971), "Incorporating Ecology into Marketing Strategy: The Case of Air Pollution," <u>Journal of Marketing</u>, 35 (July), 61-65.

Kerlinger, F. N. and E. Kaya (1970), "The Construction and Factor Analytic Validation of Scales to Measure Attitudes Toward Education," in <u>Attitude Measurement</u>, G. Summers, ed., Chicago: Rand McNally and Company, 254-64.

Kinnear, T. C. and J. R. Taylor (1973), "The Effect of Ecological Concern on Brand Perceptions," <u>Journal of Marketing Research</u>, 10 (May), 191-97.

_____, J. R. Taylor and S. A. Ahmed (1974), "Ecologically Concerned Consumers: Why Are They?" <u>Journal of Marketing</u>, 38 (April), 20-24.

Maloney, M., M. P. Ward and G. N. Braucht (1975), "A Revised Scale for the Measurement of Ecological Attitudes and Knowledge," <u>American Psychologist</u>, 30 (July), 787-90.

Mayer, R. N. (1976), "The Socially Conscious Consumer - Another Look at the Data," <u>The Journal of Consumer Research</u>, 3 (September), 113-15.

Murphy, P. E., N. Kangun and W. Locander (1978), "Environmentally Concerned Consumers - Racial Variations," <u>Journal of Marketing</u>, 42 (October), 61-66.

Nelson, J. (1974), "An Empirical Investigation of the Nature and Incidence of Ecologically Responsible Consumption of Housewives," unpublished Doctoral Disseration, University of Minnesota.

Tognacci, L., R. Weigel, M. Wideen and D. Vernon (1972), "Environmental Quality - How Universal is Public Concern?" <u>Environment and Behavior</u> (March), 73-86.

Webster, F. (1975), "Determining the Characteristics of the Socially Conscious Consumer," <u>Journal of Consumer Research</u>, 2, (December), 188-96.

IDENTIFYING THE SOCIALLY AND ECOLOGICALLY CONCERNED SEGMENT THROUGH LIFE-STYLE RESEARCH: INITIAL FINDINGS

Michael A. Belch, San Diego State University

INTRODUCTION

The effectiveness associated with segmenting markets in the private sector has been well documented, and thus accepted as a given in the formula for development of marketing strategies. The use of segmentation for purposes of creating and/or enhancing social change has not been so well documented, either as a result of few attempts to use such a strategy or lack of success in the same. In an effort to enhance social change it would seem beneficial to apply those strategies successfully employed in the private sector to the public domain. The purpose of this report is to examine the potential for making such a transition by utilizing life-style segmentation analysis for defining target markets at which socially oriented marketing programs might be targeted. More specifically, an attempt was made to identify the activities, interests, and opinions of the socially and ecologically concerned consumer.

According to Kotler (1972, p. 880) social marketing can be defined as "the design, implementation, and control of programs calculated to influence the acceptability of social ideas . . ." Generally, we think of influencing social attitudes in a sense designed to lead to benefits to individuals or society as a whole. Such programs would consider the improvement of the individual's personal well-being-- for example, personal health-- and more global or mass well-being--for example, pollution abatement. Prior attempts to segment markets on the basis of one's own personal and/or social concerns are not as common as those targeted toward the private sector. Those which have been published are generally of an exploratory nature, and as such provide so few definitive conclusions (Henion 1976). The majority of these studies examine either demographic or psychographic criteria separately, as predictor variables, and have led to conflicting results. Reizenstein (1974) for example, provides evidence that males are more concerned with their ecology than are females, while Webster (1975) indicates support for the exact opposite conslusion. Studies by Anderson, Henion and Cox (1974), Darling (1971), Shah, Turner and Willeumier (1973) and Nelson (1974) indicate that education is often a discriminator between those concerned or not concerned with ecological and social factors, while income is not. Kinnear, Taylor, and Ahmed (1974), Reizenstein, Hills, and Philpot (1974) and Webster (1975), conducting research of a similar nature, demonstrate that income may in fact be a predictor of concern while education is not--conclusions directly opposite those just reported. In reference to these same reports, age is in some instances found to be correlated with ecological concern, while in the majority of the studies it is not evidenced.

In respect to psychographic variables, Anderson, Henion, and Cox (1974) and Webster (1975) all conclude that psychological descriptors are better predictors than are demographics. A further review of these reports would seem to indicate a less than definitive conclusion, however. While Henion (1976, p. 33) indicates that ecologically concerned consumers are a subset of a more inclusive categorization of "socially concerned" consumers, and as such evidence consistent personality traits, studies by Anderson and Cunningham (1972) and Berkowitz and Daniels (1964) demonstrate agreement on such traits as conservatism, cosmopolitanism, dogmatism, and status consciousness, but opposite findings in respect to alienation, personal competency, and social responsibility. To add to the uncertainty, Kassarjian (1971) found that neither demographic nor psychographic variables discriminated between California residents concerned with air pollution.

Many of the inconsistencies in these findings can be attributed to the weaknesses associated with using personality as a criterion for segmentation (Kassarjian 1971 or 1976) and to differences in research design and sample compositions. At the same time, reports by Plummer (1974), Reynolds and Darden (1972), and Bruno, Hustad, and Pessemier (1973) among others, have demonstrated the relative advantage of considering activities, interests, and opinions over psychographic or demographic information for improving target group profiles.

The purpose of this research is to report on preliminary findings resulting from an attempt to establish a basis for segmentation of the "socially concerned" market. The segmentation criterion considered was consumers' lifestyles, with "social concern" expressed as the individuals' concern for both personal and social well-being. In respect to more specific expectations, the following propositions will be examined:

Proposition 1: In respect to activities, the more concerned individual will be more active in outdoor and physical activities than will be the less concerned counterpart.

Proposition 2: In respect to opinions, the more concerned individual will be more liberal, less dogmatic, and more self-assured than those less concerned.

Proposition 3: The more concerned individuals' interests and buying behaviors are likely to be consistent with their personal and social attitudes.

The bases underlying these propositions have been derived from a combination of those studies reviewed earlier in this review on both social and ecological consciousness and consumer lifestyles.

METHODOLOGY

Well's (1971) AIO inventory was utilized as the independent variables comprising the questionnaire. The inventory consists of 406 Likert-scaled variables designed to measure a variety of activities, interests, and opinions of the respondent. As noted by Ziff (1971) the inventory has been shown to provide an excellent insight into the psychographics and life styles of the consumer.

The social and ecological variables consisted of 20 questions designed to measure the individuals' concern over a number of dimensions including: air, noise, and water pollution; littering; the energy shortage and the future for energy; and four measures relating to one's physical health. Thus a variety of items reflective of a range of ecological and social concerns was included.

A factor analysis was performed on the 20 variables to determine the relationship between the subscales. The varimax solution yielded seven factor formations, accounting for 97.7% of the total variance, as presented in Table 1:

TABLE 1
FACTOR ANALYSIS OF SOCIAL AND ECOLOGICAL
CONCERN VARIABLES

Factor	Items	% Variance explained
Energy	4	24.7
Air Pollution	2	22.8
Exercise (Physical Health)	2	17.4
Noise Pollution	2	12.8
Water Pollution	2	8.7
Personal Habits (P.H.)	3	6.5
Attitude toward Additives (P.H.)	2	4.8

Rather than employing a test of significance for evaluating

the factor loadings, an arbitrary decision was made to use ±.30 as the cut-off point. This approach is recommended by Nunnally (1967) and is supported by Overall and Klett (1972). Perusal of the factors indicates seven distinct subscales, with all of the energy items loading on one factor, while litter was not found in any of the final formations. In addition, only three distinct physical health factors evolved.

In addition to the breakdown provided on the individual scales, total scores were computed for subsets of the dependent variables, resulting in four dimensions including a cumulative score for concern with pollution (P), energy (E), and health (H), and a total concern index (TCI) consisting of one's overall concern.

Data Collection

Students participating in a marketing research course were assigned the responsibility for data collection as part of the course requirements. Sufficient time was allotted for completing the form, as well as for minimizing bias as a result of fatigue. Measures for validating the data collection procedure were employed to insure against false information.

This procedure resulted in a usable sample of 125 individuals from representative segments of San Diego County, California. A reasonably equal proportion of males (57%) and females (43%) and a distribution among all age categories were evident.

RESULTS

Pearson product-moment correlations were computed for 406 AIO's and their relationship to the total concern index and to the individual subscales. Only those variables showing correlation coefficients significant at $p < .05$ are presented for the scales.

To facilitate presentation, the correlations will be presented in profile form with the items demonstrating significance provided in Tables 2 to 5. The profile will consist of characteristics of the individual in respect to three dimensions including opinions, social activities and interests, and consumer attitudes and behaviors.

Each table will include three sets of information including (1) the specific life style variable under consideration; (2) the coefficient of correlation (and its level of significance) between this item and the total concern index, and (3) the specific scales of concern for which significant correlations were found.

Social Activities and Interests

The social activities and interests of the concerned consumer tend to be consistent with their attitudes toward each of the dimensions considered. Table 2 provides evidence that such persons enjoy the outdoors (S1-S9), enjoy performing physical

TABLE 2

ACTIVITIES OF SOCIALLY AND ECOLOGICALLY CONCERNED CONSUMERS

Item		r Correlation between item and TCI	p	Individual Scales whose r with item was $p < .05$
S1.	I can usually work for long periods of time around the house without tiring.	.15	.05	--
S2.	I like to go for long walks.	.27	.001	E P H
S3.	I would not work if I did not have to.	-.21	.01	P H
S4.	I like to serve unusual dinners.	.19	.02	P
S5.	I am in good physical condition.	.15	.05	H
S6.	I do volunteer work for a hospital or service organization on a regular basis.	.17	.03	E H
S7.	I love the fresh air and out-of-doors.	.17	.03	E H
S8.	I like to play poker.	-.27	.002	P H
S9.	A cabin by a quiet lake is a great place to spend the summer.	.16	.05	H
S10.	I would probably be a good politician.	-.16	.04	P H
S11.	I am or have been president of a society or club.	-.17	.03	--
S12.	I do a lot of driving.	-.14	.05	P E
S13.	I would rather travel by car than by bus.	-.18	.02	P

E = Energy
H = Health
P = Pollution

activities, and are somewhat altruistic. These same individuals do not consider themselves to be swingers, and as noted in 019 can enjoy themselves without artificial stimulants. The fact that they at least espouse to do little driving and are willing to take the bus further demonstrates consistency between their ecological and social concerns and their activities. The remaining items reflect the desire to engage in physical activities as opposed to those of a formalized and less physical nature. Participation in and leadership of clubs or social organizations does not seem to be a preference among those high in social and ecological concern.

In summary, the activities of the concerned individual appear to be consistent with their attitudes. These individuals seem to participate in activities that will allow them to be outdoors or philanthropic, and to shy away from those that require formal structure and confinement.

Opinions

Tables 3 and 4 reflect the fact that the individual scoring

TABLE 3

OPINIONS OF SOCIALLY AND ECOLOGICALLY CONCERNED CONSUMERS

Item	r Correlation between item and TCI	p	Individual Scales whose r with item was $p < .05$
01. Generally speaking women are less intelligent than men.	-.24	.004	P
02. The father should be the boss in the house.	-.24	.004	E P
03. A woman's most important activities and interests tend to be ones which her husband cannot participate in.	-.26	.002	P
04. A woman's place is in the home.	-.19	.02	P H
05. Women are usually poor drivers.	-.21	.01	P H
06. Women should be free to take jobs outside the home if they want them.	.16	.05	P
07. Women wear too much make-up these days.	-.16	.05	P H
08. Blacks and whites understand each other less today than they did five years ago.	-.14	.05	E
09. I would never live next to someone of a different race.	-.17	.03	P H
010. It seems that black people are getting more opportunities today than they deserve.	-.31	.001	E P
011. A woman should have important interests outside the home, whether it is a job, community activity or church work.	.21	.005	E P H

E = Energy
H = Health
P = Pollution

TABLE 4

OPINIONS OF SOCIALLY AND ECOLOGICALLY
CONCERNED CONSUMERS - ROLES

Item		r Correlation between item and TCI	p	Individual Scales whose r with item was p < .05
012.	Nobody cares what I think.	-.15	.05	P
013.	Everyone should use mouthwash.	-.20	.01	H
014.	I often wish for the good old days.	-.19	.02	E P
015.	Most people should mind their own business.	-.32	.001	E P H
016.	Spiritual values are more important than material things.	.22	.009	P H
017.	Our family is too heavily in debt today.	-.15	.05	E H
018.	I would like to be a professional football player.	-.21	.01	P H
019.	A party wouldn't be a party without liquor.	-.21	.01	E H
020.	I would be willing to pay higher taxes to get better public transportation.	.15	.05	P
021.	Five years from now, the family income will probably be a lot higher than it is now.	-.16	.05	P
022.	It is more important to live graciously than it is to save up a lot of money for the future.	-.19	.01	P H
023.	These days you have to take things as they come; you can't plan ahead.	-.23	.005	E P
024.	I would pay $15 more on my income tax for a program of Federal pollution control.	.30	.001	E P H

E = Energy
H = Health
P = Pollution

high on the TCI is likely to be more liberal, open-minded, and perhaps more secure than his(her) less concerned counterpart. Items 01 to 07 demonstrate the concern for equality of roles between men and women, while 08 and 010 reflect a liberal stance regarding those of another race. In addition, the remaining miscellaneous items portray the concerned individual as secure and cognizant of his role in society. Such individuals are less likely to accept the status quo, feel that the future is likely to be less than ideal, and are willing to give (at least financially) to work toward improvement.

The last five items (020-024) indicate that, while the

concerned individual may feel less than certain about the future, she/he is not resigned to the fact that improvements are not possible. Such persons feel that, while their financial status is not necessarily likely to improve, it is possible to plan, it is possible to get ahead financially, and detrimental and/or ecological conditions are not inevitable.

In summary, concerned consumers tend to be financially and emotionally secure, uncertain about the future, but willing to accept the responsibility to improve the same. The liberal posture tends to be supported by a number of activities in which these persons engage.

Consumer Attitudes and Behaviors

Perhaps of prime interest to the marketer are the attitudes and behaviors of the concerned consumer in respect to consumption patterns and the corporate world in general. A more thorough understanding of these specific behaviors would allow for greater planning and development of marketing mix strategies. When considered along with the financial variables considered in Table 4, Table 5 provides an interesting profile of this

TABLE 5

CONSUMPTION PATTERNS OF SOCIALLY AND ECOLOGICALLY CONCERNED CONSUMERS

Item	r Correlation between item and TCI	p	Individual Scales whose r with item was p <.05
C1. It is important to have a good looking car.	-.22	.007	P H
C2. I am more concerned with a products appearance than its durability.	-.20	.01	E P
C3. I like new cars better than old cars.	-.34	.001	E P H
C4. If a car functions properly, it doesn't matter how a car looks.	.16	.05	P
C5. The new styles turn me on.	-.17	.03	P H
C6. I am interested in cars.	-.25	.003	P H
C7. I am usually the first in the family to suggest that we get a new car.	-.34	.001	E P H
C8. I know a lot about the mechanical aspects of cars.	-.26	.002	P H
C9. The man should have the final say on what car to buy.	-.34	.001	P H
C10. I buy many things with a credit card or charge card.	-.26	.002	E H P

TABLE 5 (continued)

CONSUMPTION PATTERNS OF SOCIALLY AND ECOLOGICALLY
CONCERNED CONSUMERS

Item		r Correlation between item and TCI	p	Individual Scales whose r with item was p < .05
C11.	I would like to have a maid to do the housework.	-.15	.05	E H
C12.	I would like to own the most expensive things.	-.24	.004	P H
C13.	I would like to own and fly my own airplane.	-.20	.01	H
C14.	A person can save a lot of money by shopping around for bargains.	.17	.03	P
C15.	I keep away from unfamiliar brands.	.21	.01	H P
C16.	At the grocery store, I buy just about the same items week after week.	.17	.03	P
C17.	I do most of my grocery shopping in one store.	.15	.05	E
C18.	Advertising should give us more factual information.	.19	.02	P H
C19.	If a product is not safe and reliable, it does not stay on the market for a long time.	-.24	.005	E P
C20.	Most big companies are just out for themselves.	-.16	.05	E H
C21.	I try not to eat foods that are high in cholesterol.	.26	.002	E H
C22.	The gasoline engine is harmful to us all.	.15	.05	P H
C23.	I serve some foods because they have certain health benefits.	.23	.006	H P
C24.	Ready-to-serve foods are important because they let you save time for more important activities than cooking.	-.29	.001	E P H
C25.	Small economical cars will be more popular in the future than they are now.	.20	.02	E P H
C26.	Now is a good time to buy a car.	-.26	.002	E P H
C27.	Pollution is the inevitable price of progress.	-.22	.008	P
C28.	American made is best made.	-.31	.001	E P

E = Energy
H = Health
P = Pollution

target segment. Besides being financially stable, the concerned individual is seemingly not sold on the idea that now is a good time to purchase, that American-made is necessarily best, or that things will not get better in the future in respect to products and their effect on the environment. Items C1 to C5 indicate a more rational buyer whose concerns are with functional product attributes as opposed to appearance, style, or newness. In respect to automobiles these individuals seem almost to be disinterested or uninvolved (C6-C9).

In many respects, the concerned consumer appears to be conservative regarding consumption habits. Besides being a rational buyer, these persons prefer to pay with cash and dislike using credit cards for anything other than major purchases. The luxuries of life seem to be of little importance (C11-C13), bargains and price deals are sought, and both brand and store loyalty is evident (C16-C17). There appears to be no consistent pattern emerging with respect to attitudes toward business and advertising in general (C18-C20). As noted with the activities engaged in by this group, the consumption patterns do appear to be consistent with their attitudes toward the social and ecological environment. Items C21-C24 indicate that purchases of products that are harmful or of a convenience nature are less preferred than those likely to provide more positive benefits.

SUMMARY AND CONCLUSIONS

Based on the profiles provided in this study, it is now possible to draw a more complete profile of socially and environmentally concerned consumers. The segment of the population most likely to be concerned with ecological problems, energy supplies, and physical well-being can best be characterized as more liberal, more self-assured of their present and future status, and more socially and physically active than their less concerned counterparts, supporting the three propositions under examination. In addition, their life-styles and consumption activities are consistent with their attitudes toward the dimensions considered.

When combining the results of this study with those reviewed earlier, a more complete profile is possible. In total, the individual demonstrating concern for ecological and social conditions can be characterized as:

> A young male or female of the higher strata in respect to income, education, and socio-economic standing in general. Such persons are more open-minded, liberal and secure than those demonstrating less concern, and are likely to be rational and conservative in respect to their consuming behaviors. Both the activities and products of consumption of this segment are consistent with their attitudes regarding personal well-

being, society, and the ecology.

The implications of such findings should be evident. It is now possible to proceed beyond the previously utilized demographic and personality profiles established in earlier studies to the point where the marketing mix strategies can be directed to a more specific target audience. As evidenced by successes in the private sector, the net result is likely to be more efficient employment of social change strategies, with an increased probability of effectiveness of the same (Henion has previously established the fact that a market of concerned consumers satisfies the requirements of employing a strategy of segmentation (as set forth by Kotler (1972)).

Finally, it is necessary to discuss limitations of the study. While the results of this research are interesting and quite revealing, they must be treated as tentative. The relatively small sample size and specific geographic location limit the generalizability of the results to other populations. In addition, it would be interesting to factor analyze the AIO data to ascertain whether the factor scores that result provide similar conclusions to those derived in this research when correlated with the dependent variables. The size of the sample and number of variables considered limit the possibility of such a strategy, however, signifying a need for additional data collection.

Such limitations notwithstanding, the study does contribute to our understanding of the lifestyles of the socially and ecologically concerned consumer. Additional data collection in this regard is now in progress and will be analyzed to support or refute conclusions made in this initial study that future attempts to identify socially and ecologically concerned consumers should make use of life-style segmentation as a social change strategy.

REFERENCES

Anderson, W. T. and W.H. Cunningham (1972), "The Socially Conscious Consumer," *Journal of Marketing*, 36 (July), 22-31.

_____, K. E. Henion and E. P. Cox (1974), "Socially vs. Ecologically Responsible Consumers," *AMA Combined Conference Proceedings*, 36 (Spring and Fall), 304-311.

Bruno, A., T. Hustad and E. Pessemier (1973), "Media Approaches to Segmentation," *Journal of Advertising Research*, 13 (April), 35-43.

Darling, J. R. (1971), "Consumer Perception of the Pollution Problem: A Research Study," unpublished.

Henion, Karl E. (1976), *Ecological Marketing*, Columbus: Grid Books.

Kassarjian, H. H. (1971a), "Personality and Consumer Behavior: A Review," *Journal of Marketing Research*, 8 (Nov.), 409-418.

_____ (1971b), "Incorporating Ecology Into Marketing Strategy: The Case of Air Pollution," *Journal of Marketing*, 35 (July) 61-65.

Kotler, Philip (1972), *Marketing Management: Analysis, Planning and Control*, 2nd edition, Englewood Cliffs: Prentice-Hall.

Nelson, J.E. (1974), "An Empirical Investigation of the Nature & Incidence of Ecologically Responsible Consumption of Housewives," unpublished doctoral dissertation, U. of Minnesota.

Nunnally, J. (1967), *Psychometric Theory*, New York: McGraw Hill.

Overall, J. E. and Klett, C. J. (1972) *Applied Multivariate Analysis*, New York: McGraw Hill.

Peters, W. H. (1974), "Who Cooperates in Voluntary Recycling Efforts?", *American Marketing Association Combined Conference Proceedings*, 36 (Spring and Fall), 323-328.

Plummer, J. T. (1974), "The Concept and Application of Life Style Segmentation," *Journal of Marketing*, 38 (Jan.), 33-37.

Reizenstein, R. G., G. E. Hills and J. W. Philpot (1973), "Willingness to Pay for Control of Air Pollution: A Demographic Analysis," *American Marketing Association Combined Conference Proceedings*, series 35 (Spring and Fall) 482-485.

Reynolds, F. and W. Darden (1972), "Intermarket Patronage: A Psychographic Study of Consumer Outshoppers," *Journal of Marketing*, 36 (October), 50-54.

Shah, Pankaj, R.E. Turner and S. Willeumier (1973), "Attitudes Toward Business: A Comparison of Factor Structures," *American Marketing Association Combined Conference Proceedings*, series 35 (Spring and Fall), 482-485.

Webster, F. E. (1975), "Determining the Characteristics of the Socially Conscious Consumer," *Journal of Consumer Research*, 2 (December), 188-195.

Wells, W. D. and D. J. Tigert (1971), "Activities, Interests and Opinions," *Journal of Advertising Research*, 11 (August), 27-35.

Ziff, R. (1971), "Psychographics for Market Segmentation," *Journal of Advertising Research*, 11 (April), 3-9.

AN ATTITUDINAL AND A BEHAVIORAL
INDEX OF ENERGY CONSERVATION

Patrick E. Murphy, Gene R. Laczniak,
and Richard K. Robinson
Marquette University

INTRODUCTION

The necessity for prolonged energy conservation in the U.S. is once again well established by lengthening gasoline lines and the serious concerns of oil companies and government over the sufficiency of fuel supplies. There is still a need for more knowledge of how consumers have reacted to the increasingly common "tight energy" situation. Several questions come to mind: What are consumers' attitudes toward the energy problem in the U.S.? How closely are their attitudes related to their consumption behavior? Is it possible to develop an index of energy conservation based on both attitudinal and behavioral components? What are the socioeconomic characteristics of those who are most sensitive to energy conservation?

A survey of energy consumers in an energy-dependent Northern state was conducted to provide at least partial answers to the above questions. Another aim of this research was to again compare the consumer's perception of the energy crisis with that of local utilities, which has been reported elsewhere (Laczniak, Murphy and Robinson 1978; Robinson, Murphy and Laczniak 1979). Before discussing the methodology and findings of the study, a brief analysis of the relationship between energy conservation and consumer behavior is provided as background.

ENERGY CONSERVATION AND CONSUMER BEHAVIOR

Prior research on the effect of the energy shortage on human behavior has yielded mixed results. Curtin (1976) found in a 1974 nationwide sample that "More than half of all respondents said that they had reduced their consumption at least 'somewhat' below the prior year's level for each classification--home heating, electricity and gasoline. Less than one respondent in five reported no conservation at all" (p. 40). In a study of four Texas counties, Gottlieb and Matre (1976) concluded that few of their respondents felt there was a serious energy crisis in 1974 and those who could afford it did not engage in any conservation behavior at that time. Finally, Milstein's (1977) findings suggested that the public is not willing to sacrifice comfort and convenience because of the energy situation.

In a recent conceptual article on energy and consumer behavior, Shanklin (1978) stated that energy consumption patterns of Americans are largely habitual and based on a lifetime of learning. The attitudes underlying such energy behavior are often deeply ingrained. Thus, the attitude-behavior linkage appears central to an understanding of consumers' energy conservation stance.

One way to investigate different levels of consumer sensitivity to an issue is to develop an "index" of concern toward the issue. Kinnear and Taylor (1973) developed such an index of ecological concern. Their index contained both attitudinal and behavioral dimensions. They found that "the higher a buyer's ecological concern, the more salient is the ecological dimension in perception, and the greater is the perceived similarity of brands that are ecologically non-distinctive" (p. 196).

A variation of this type of index was constructed to try to illuminate factors that influence energy conservation.

METHODOLOGY

During November, 1977 consumers in Wisconsin were contacted via a mail survey. Four hundred residents of Milwaukee and 360 inhabitants of Madison were selected at random from street address/telephone directories and sent a four-page questionnaire. Questions focused on attitudes and actual behavior of consumers toward energy conservation, including general opinions about the energy problem and statements of personal commitment to conserving it.

The return rate for the Milwaukee sample was higher than that for the Madison sample, with 231 respondents from Milwaukee (58%) and 158 respondents from Madison (45%) returning completed questionnaires. There was a good dispersion of respondents across most demographic categories; the typical respondent was a middle-income working male, young to middle-aged, married with a small family. The only significant inter-sample difference between respondents in the two cities was in educational level. As might be expected, since Madison is a white-collar town, (university city and state capital), 76 percent of the Madison sample had attained at least some college education versus 59 percent for the Milwaukee sample.

FINDINGS

Since the energy problem in the U.S. is complex, a single index combining both attitudinal and behavioral components, as Kinnear and Taylor (1973) had constructed for ecological concern, was considered inappropriate in the present case. Instead, two separate indices were developed for each component. With this approach it is possible to explore the attitude-behavior relationship so often discussed in the consumer behavior literature.

Table 1 shows the frequency distributions for both the behavioral and attitudinal indices. Specific index questions and corresponding point values for the answers are presented in the appendix. Since these questions compose the building blocks of the energy index, the interested reader should review

TABLE 1

FREQUENCY DISTRIBUTIONS OF SCORES ON ENERGY CONSERVATION INDICES

Score	Attitude Index Frequency	(%)	Behavioral Index Frequency	(%)
-7			1	.3
-6			1	.3
-5			4	1.0
-4			2	.5
-3			4	1.0
-2			17	4.4
-1			21	5.4
0			21	5.4
1	1	.3	37	9.5
2			53	13.6
3	7	1.8	44	11.3
4	12	3.1	41	10.5
5	27	6.9	48	12.3
6	65	16.7	32	8.2
7	102	26.2	34	8.7
8	82	21.1	15	3.9
9	61	15.7	7	1.8
10	22	5.7	2	.5
11	9	2.3	2	.5
12	1	.3	3	.8
Total	389	99.8	389	99.9

the appendix at this time. The possible range of score values for the attitudinal index is narrower than that of the behavioral because the former has fewer questions.

For analytical purposes, the scores were divided into three groups for each scale, indicating <u>low,</u> <u>moderate</u> and <u>high</u> levels of energy conservation. For the attitudinal index, the division was accomplished by assigning the two modal values of 7 and 8, around which scores concentrated, to the moderate category. Scores 1 to 6 were assigned to the low category; scores 9 to 12, to the high category.

For the behavioral index, the division of scores into three manageable groups was done by assigning scores 2 to 5 to the moderate category. Scores equal to or less than 1 were assigned to the low category; scores 6 or more, to the high category. The break between low/moderate was put at 1 rather than at 0 in order to keep the percentage of respondents in the low category similar to the corresponding percentage for the attitudinal index. (Answers to part or all of questions 3, 4 and 6 were negatively scored because the indicated behavior was considered wasteful of energy. The 68°F answer has the zero point in question 3 since the federal government has advocated that thermostats be set at this temperature in winter.)

For the attitudinal energy conservation index, Table 2 shows the frequencies (and chi square results) cross-tabulated by score category and demographic characteristics. Age, marital status, persons living in the household, and family income were not significantly related to index scores. Education and occupation level, however, were significantly associated with these scores.

Persons who hold a college degree or have done post-baccalaureate work were more likely to be labeled "high" on the index than their less-educated counterparts. The significant result for occupation was not surprising since this characteristic is usually correlated with education. Thus, the blue collar and unskilled occupational segment tended to score lower on the index.

Social class, which was computed by the Hollingshead Two-Factor Index of Social Position, was also related to attitudinal values. Since the two factors utilized were education and occupation of the household head, a significant relationship was expected. In particular, upper-social-class respondents were found to be significantly more energy-conservation conscious than middle- or lower-class respondents.

TABLE 2

FREQUENCIES BY DEMOGRAPHIC CHARACTERISTIC AND SCORE CATEGORY
FOR ATTITUDINAL ENERGY CONSERVATION INDEX

Demographic characteristic	Score category		
	Low	Moderate	High
Age			
Young (34 or less)	39	62	36
Middle-aged (35-54)	35	77	32
Older (55 or over)	37	42	22
	111	181	90
x^2=5.78			
Marital Status			
Single	14	25	16
Married	83	135	60
Divorced/widowed	15	23	14
	112	183	90
x^2=1.97			
Persons in Household			
1	13	21	14
2-3	62	91	44
4-5	28	56	24
6 or more	6	13	8
	109	181	90
x^2=3.16			
Education Level			
Some high school or less	7	12	6
High school grad & some college	70	101	34
College grad or more	32	67	49
	109	180	89
x^2=14.94[b] (overall); 14.2[a] (College grad--less than college grad)			
Occupation Level			
Professional & managerial (P/M)	6	34	18
Other white collar & clerical (OWC/CL)	50	85	49
Blue collar & unskilled (BC/U)	46	53	19
	102	172	86
x^2=17.97[a] (overall); 17.5[a] (P/M-OWC/CL); 16.3[a] (P/M-BC/U); 14.3[a] (OWC/CL-BC/U)			

TABLE 2 (continued)

Demographic characteristic	Score category		
	Low	Moderate	High
Income			
Less than $10,000	19	25	13
$10,000-19,999	36	66	29
$20,000 and over	36	64	38
	91	155	80
$x^2=2.08$			
Social Class			
Upper	6	31	15
Middle	70	110	58
Lower	26	33	13
	102	174	86

$x^2=10.12^c$ (overall); 7.08^c (Upper-Middle); 9.76^b (Upper-Lower); 1.76 (Middle-Lower)

[a] Significant at .001 level.
[b] Significant at .01 level.
[c] Significant at .05 level.

For the behavioral energy conservation index, frequencies were also cross-tabulated by score category and demographic characteristic. Although those who scored "high" on the energy conservation index showed some tendency to be young, married, from small families and of the middle social class (i.e., white collar and moderate educational level), no significant relationships were found and hence the cross tabulations are not shown. The findings support the view that the public's behavior patterns with respect to energy conservation are lagging behind their stated attitudes.

To study the attitude-behavior issue, the two indices were compared to one another in Table 3. One would expect the numbers on the diagonal to be the highest if attitudes are a good predictor of energy-conserving behavior. As can be seen in the table, only for the moderate category of conservation concern are attitudes good predictors of behavior. For the extremes, the attitudinal index is not a particularly good predictor of energy conservation behavior.

CONCLUSIONS AND IMPLICATIONS

The most obvious conclusion that can be drawn from these

TABLE 3

FREQUENCIES BY SCORE CATEGORY FOR ATTITUDINAL
AND BEHAVIORAL INDICES

Score category for attitudinal index	Score category for behavioral index		
	Low	Moderate	High
Low	40	50	22
Moderate	48	93	43
High	20	43	30
	108	186	95

$x^2 = 8.09$[a]

[a]Significant at .05 level.

findings is that, for the two indices constructed in this research, the attitude-behavior linkage regarding energy conservation is not a strong one. Although individuals classified upper social class (i.e., high educational and occupational levels) were significantly more likely to score "high" on the attitudinal index, their behavioral index scores did not differ significantly from those of members of the other classes. Upper-class persons have likely talked and read more about the energy shortage and probably can identify the issues surrounding it. However, they may not feel that the financial or psychic rewards associated with a behavioral change are worth the inconvenience.

Results of this study have implications for managers and public policy makers. Energy marketers need to increasingly segment their appeals to distinct demographic groups. For instance, the upper-social-class person who already holds a positive attitude toward energy conservation needs to be supplied information about meaningful actions that he or she can take to translate existing attitudes into behavior. Possibly, a print advertising campaign which discusses societal benefits associated with specific energy-conserving behavior may be effective in reaching this group. The rationale for this approach has been argued in the literature (Brooker 1976); namely, that upper-social-class individuals tend to engage in environmentally self-actualizing behavior.

Approaches to consumers in the middle and lower social classes should be different. Since they did not score as high on the attitudinal index, more of an educationally oriented campaign may be necessary to gain enduring commitment to energy conservation. Television advertising may represent the best media vehicle to dramatically reach this segment with the message that a commitment to energy conservation is important. Specifically, these consumers should be informed about which conserving actions yield the greatest financial benefits (i.e., dollar savings) to the individual.

Public policy makers need to take more drastic measures to bring about energy conservation. Since the data for this project were collected in late 1977, consumers were obviously not feeling enough pressure to significantly alter their behavior. A policy position more consonant with today's mounting problems is one that implicitly attempts to reverse the direction of the attitude-to-behavior flow. Thus, through consumption disincentives such as taxes, price hikes and rationing, policy makers should strive to bring about changes in behavior first. In this way evolving governmental influence could alter the traditional model to a behavior-to-attitude one. This point could be underscored by having advertisements illustrate how energy-saving actions of other consumers have led to saving money and/or societal benefits. By being "forced" to change their behavior, consumers will probably change their attitudes and become more favorably disposed to energy conservation, thereby making subsequent energy-conserving actions easier to undertake.

APPENDIX

INDICES

Attitudinal Energy Conservation Index

1. How important a problem do you consider energy to be in the U.S. today?

   0 not important
   1 slightly important
   2 moderately important
   3 extremely important
   4 the most important problem

2. How committed are you to conserving energy?

   3 extremely committed
   2 moderately committed
   1 slightly committed
   0 neutral
   -1 slightly uncommitted
   -2 moderately uncommitted
   -3 extremely uncommitted

3. How much impact will your conservation efforts have in the future on total energy conservation?
   3 great deal
   2 moderate
   1 little
   0 no impact

4. Do you believe that you are doing all that you can to conserve energy?
   0 yes
   2 no
   1 don't know

Behavioral Energy Conservation Index

1. If currently employed, how do you commute to work the majority of the time?

    <u>1</u> carpool
    <u>2</u> ride the bus
    <u>0</u> drive alone in a car, van or truck
    <u>2</u> ride a motorcycle
    <u>3</u> ride a bicycle or walk

2. Are you making fewer trips by car these days to shop or run errands in order to conserve energy?

    <u>1</u> yes
    <u>0</u> no

3. During the day in the heating season what temperature do you set the thermostat on?

    <u>2</u> 64° or less
    <u>1</u> 65°-67°
    <u>0</u> 68°
    <u>-1</u> 69°-70°
    <u>-2</u> 71° or over

4. If you own an air conditioner, do you consider your family's use of air conditioning to be

    <u>-3</u> heavy user
    <u>-2</u> moderate user
    <u>-1</u> light user

5. Which of the following steps have you taken to reduce energy consumption in your residence? (check <u>all</u> that apply)

    <u>1</u> turn heat down at night
    <u>1</u> shut off heat in unused rooms
    <u>1</u> turn off lights when not in room
    <u>1</u> less outside lighting (e.g., decorative outdoor lights)
    <u>1</u> turn down water heater temperature
    <u>1</u> run dishwasher with fuller loads or less often
    <u>1</u> run washer and dryer at night or on weekends
    <u>1</u> reduce use of air conditioning
    <u>1</u> reduce use of other electrical appliances (TV, stereo, radio, etc.)

6. Please check the electrical appliances that your family owns and <u>uses</u> regularly.

    <u>-1</u> electric can opener
    <u>-1</u> electric TV antenna
    <u>-1</u> 3 or more TV's
    <u>-1</u> blow dryer
    <u>-1</u> electric hair roller set
    <u>-1</u> electric garage door opener
    <u>-1</u> electric lawn hedge trimmer

REFERENCES

Brooker, George (1976), "The Self-Actualizing Socially Conscious Consumer," *Journal of Consumer Research*, 3 (September), 107-112.

Curtin, Richard T. (1976), "Consumer Adaptation to Energy Shortages," *Journal of Energy and Development*, (Autumn) 38-59.

Gottlieb, David and Marc Matre (1976), "Conceptions of Energy Shortages and Energy Conserving Behavior," *Social Science Quarterly*, (September), 421-429.

Kinnear, Thomas C. and James R. Taylor (1973), "The Effect of Ecological Concerns on Brand Perceptions," *Journal of Marketing Research*, 10 (May), 191-197.

Laczniak, Gene R., Patrick E. Murphy and Richard K. Robinson (1978), "Evaluating the Marketing of Energy Conservation by Utilities," *Akron Business and Economics Review*, 3 (Fall), 6-10.

Milstein, Jeffrey S. (1977), "Attitudes, Knowledge and Behavior of American Consumers with Some Implication for Government Action," in *Advances in Consumer Research*, William D. Perreault, Jr., ed., Atlanta: Association for Consumer Research.

Robinson, Richard K., Patrick E. Murphy and Gene R. Laczniak (1979), "The Energy Problem: Consumers' and Utilities' Views with Marketing Implications," in *Developments in Marketing Science*, Vol. II, Howard S. Gitlow and Edward W. Whertley, eds., Miami, FL: Academy of Marketing Science.

Shanklin, William L. (1978), "The Energy Crisis and Consumer Behavior," *Atlanta Economic Review*, 28 (May-June), 28-32.

CONSUMER ENERGY PATTERNS IN CANADA:
INDICATORS FOR THE CONSERVER SOCIETY[1]

J. R. Brent Ritchie, The University of Calgary
John D. Claxton, University of British Columbia
Gordon H. G. McDougall, Wilfrid Laurier University

INTRODUCTION

One of the major components of a conserver society is "doing more with less" (Shapiro 1978). The notion is based on the premise that a considerable amount of waste exists in our present system. By reducing the waste through a more enlightened policy of resource management and use, people can actually do more and yet consume less resources. A central issue of a conserver society model is the willingness of the general public to adopt the behaviors necessary to accomplish the goals. A practical "test" of this willingness is now available-- consumers' reactions to the energy situation.

Since the oil embargo of 1973, considerable publicity has been given to the dwindling supply of energy resources in the world, particularly oil. In the view of conservers, the effect of the cheap energy strategy in North America has created a wasteful lifestyle. The present issue is whether that lifestyle can be altered to reflect the environmental necessity of more effective and efficient utilization of energy. Because of the publicity surrounding this issue, consumer reaction to the energy situation could be the basis for a forecast of the probability of adopting conserver modes.

This paper will discuss the conserver society within the context of usage of energy by the consumer. It has two broad objectives;

1. to discuss the purpose and methodology of a national study designed to provide base-line knowledge about energy consumption and conservation

---

[1]The authors express their appreciation to the Department of Consumer and Corporate Affairs Canada for the financial support which made possible the study on which this paper is based.

practices (EECP) of Canadian households.

2. to provide initial results from the study on Canadian household attitudes, knowledge and behaviors towards energy.

The present study is only one of several pieces of research being conducted on this topic within the framework of the overall Energy Research and Development activities of the Government of Canada (EMR 1977). Its undertaking is part of a sub-program responsible for determining how the amounts and types of energy used by consumers can be reduced so as to contribute to the achievement of Canada's energy conservation goals (EMR 1978).

SCOPE AND OBJECTIVES OF THE RESEARCH

The aim of this study is to provide researchers and policy makers with an in-depth description and understanding of the energy consumption and conservation patterns (ECCP) of Canadian households. This aim is considered an essential first step in the development of policies and programs designed to modify such patterns. The significance of the term "patterns" is to draw attention to the interrelated nature of household energy consumption and conservation, which actually are part of an integrated life style. The focus is not on individual <u>components</u> but on <u>patterns</u> of energy consumption and conservation.

EECP has a broader interpretation than just household energy behaviors and refers to what householders know, think, and prefer, as well as what they do. In other words, the term refers to patterns of knowledge, views, values, and behaviors.

In three major sections, this paper will discuss the initial phases of the program of ECCP research. The remainder of this section reviews its major purposes, background concerns, and conceptual development that provided its initial structure. This is followed by a section that discusses development of the data base. The final section presents preliminary conclusions and indicates future directions for ECCP study.

<u>Research Purposes</u>

These were twofold:

- to describe household energy consumption and conservation patterns in order to help consumers become more aware of the importance of energy conservation.

- to understand household energy consumption and conservation patterns in order to assist in the evaluation of energy conservation policies.

The first purpose, aimed at increasing the energy awareness of consumers, is based on two premises: (1) consumers do not see energy supplies as a major concern at present, and (2) their understanding of energy consumption is hampered by a lack of factual information about their own consumption relative to that of their neighbours and consumers in other parts of Canada. The implication for ECCP research is that an integrated picture of household energy consumption is needed in order to provide consumers with a straight forward means of putting their own consumption into perspective.

The second purpose was aimed at helping in the evaluation of energy policies. Clearly consumers represent a major potential target for energy policy efforts. Examples of policy alternatives include restricting energy-consuming products, persuading consumers to reduce consumption, increasing energy prices, and subsidizing energy-conserving products. From a conserver standpoint, the goal is to avoid most of these policy alternatives and have the required change in energy-use patterns result from consumer recognition of and appreciation for efficient and effective energy use.

From the perspective of policy selection, it is possible to assess, in a technical sense, the energy savings that could result from any particular policy. However, consumer reaction to the policy will influence the degree to which _potential_ savings become _actual_ savings. Once again, an integrated picture of household energy consumption is needed. This picture should show not only factual information as to types and amounts of energy consumed, but also information regarding consumer feelings about the importance of various energy-consuming activities. How much energy is consumed in various household areas? In which areas would consumers be most willing to reduce energy use? What types of energy restrictions would consumers find least objectionable? Which consumers will be most affected? Questions of this type are addressed during the formulation and selection of energy conservation policy. Answers to such questions require a thorough understanding of household ECCP.

Background Concerns

Three concerns motivated and guided the development of the ECCP research. The first was the evidence of impending energy shortages. The second was evidence showing consumers did not feel a need to reduce energy consumption significantly. The third concern was a framework for energy conservation policy that was being developed by the Canadian Department of Consumer and Corporate Affairs (Evans, Ritchie and McDougall 1978).

"Energy shortages" concerns. Notwithstanding the apparent abundance of energy resources currently available to Canadians, serious energy shortages must be faced in the not-too-distant future. A stark reminder is provided by Energy Futures for Canadians, a report published by the federal department of Energy, Mines and Resources (1978). It indicates that if Canada is to be self-reliant in energy by the year 2000 all of the following must occur:

- reduce energy demand growth rate to one-half of the 5.3 percent historic rate;
- increase Canadian oil production by 50 percent;
- increase natural gas production by one-third;
- increase coal production by four to five times;
- increase electrical energy from one-third to one-half of total primary energy; and
- supply at least 5 percent of primary energy from renewables (other than hydro).

A major recommendation of the above report was the establishment of an Energy Information and Participation Program. Three program objectives parallel the purposes of the current ECCP research, namely:

- ensure that the public is aware of the national threat posed by the evolving energy situation in Canada and abroad and is continually able to evaluate the implications of changing developments;
- assist members of the public to appreciate how their active, responsible participation in energy-related

activities contributes to a satisfactory energy transformation; and

- ensure that up-to-date information is always available to participants in all parts of the country to permit meaningful discussion, debate, evaluation and participation in energy-related programs.

<u>"I'm alright, Jack" concerns</u>. A number of factors had helped form consumers' opinions about the seriousness of the energy shortages. The 1973 oil embargo and subsequent shortages prompted many Canadians to realize that energy supplies should not be taken for granted. However, more recent oil discoveries, disagreements between governments and industry as to reserve levels, and the apparent lack of any major conservation initiatives have resulted in consumer confusion and complacency over household conservation efforts.

Evidence of dwindling consumer interest in conservation was provided by a longitudinal study commissioned by the Office of Energy Conservation, Department of Energy, Mines and Resources. Consumer perceptions of the seriousness of the energy shortage gradually increased from 1975 through 1977. However, this trend reversed in 1978 when consumers considered energy shortages to be less serious than they had the year before (McDougall and Keller 1979).

Other evidence was provided by a pilot survey conducted at the outset of the current study. It indicated consumers were largely unaware of how their household energy consumption compared with other households. Even households with extremely high consumption levels felt they had "about the same" as other households. Further, most consumers felt they were doing as much for energy conservation as most other people. The phrase "I'm alright, Jack" describes this apparently common attitude toward conservation. It is antithetical to the conserver society.

Concern over this prevailing attitude led ECCP researchers to look for ways to use the findings of the study to increase consumer awareness. One way was to summarize major types of household energy consumption by means of a profile indicating consumption of home energy and gasoline.

<u>Energy conservation policy concerns</u>. Meanwhile, a framework for analysis and formulation of energy policy was being constructed concurrently with the development of the

ECCP study program. The purpose of the framework was to provide (1) a means of enumerating energy conservation policies and (2) a structure for cataloging conservation research information. A major outcome of this structure was the concept of a "pay-off matrix". It identified the energy saved by each policy of the policy framework. For example, what is the potential energy saving caused by increasing home insulation or shifting from frost-free to manual defrost refrigerators? Substantial progress has been made towards successful completion of a pay-off matrix that will provide answers to such questions (Cullen 1978).

Matrix pay-offs were defined on a <u>technical</u> basis. It remained for ECCP research to assess consumer views and preferences regarding various types of energy, energy applications, and government actions. Understanding consumer "energy values" was seen as critical to the task of judging consumer reaction to any policy alternatives, and hence the extent to which <u>actual</u> energy savings would match <u>potential</u> energy savings.

In summary, three background concerns shaped the ECCP research. "Energy shortages" concerns provided the major impetus for the study. The "I'm alright, Jack" outlook of consumers focused attention on means of increasing consumer sensitivity to household energy consumption. This in turn suggested the concept of household energy consumption profiles. Finally, conservation policy concerns prompted ECCP research to examine not only consumption information, but also links between energy consumption and household energy values.

Development of ECCP Research

Before developing the research methodology, attention was directed at three areas of conceptual importance. The first was the formulation of a model of factors that might influence household energy consumption and conservation decisions. The second was the development of the concept of a household energy consumption profile. The final area was the evaluation of possible measurement problems associated with obtaining information on household energy consumption.

<u>Household energy decision model</u>. Figure 1 presents the heuristic model that was developed to guide the collection and analysis of the data. The bottom half of the model identifies three major sets of dependent (or resultant) variables. One set is behavioral, dealing with ongoing household consumption and conservation actions. The two

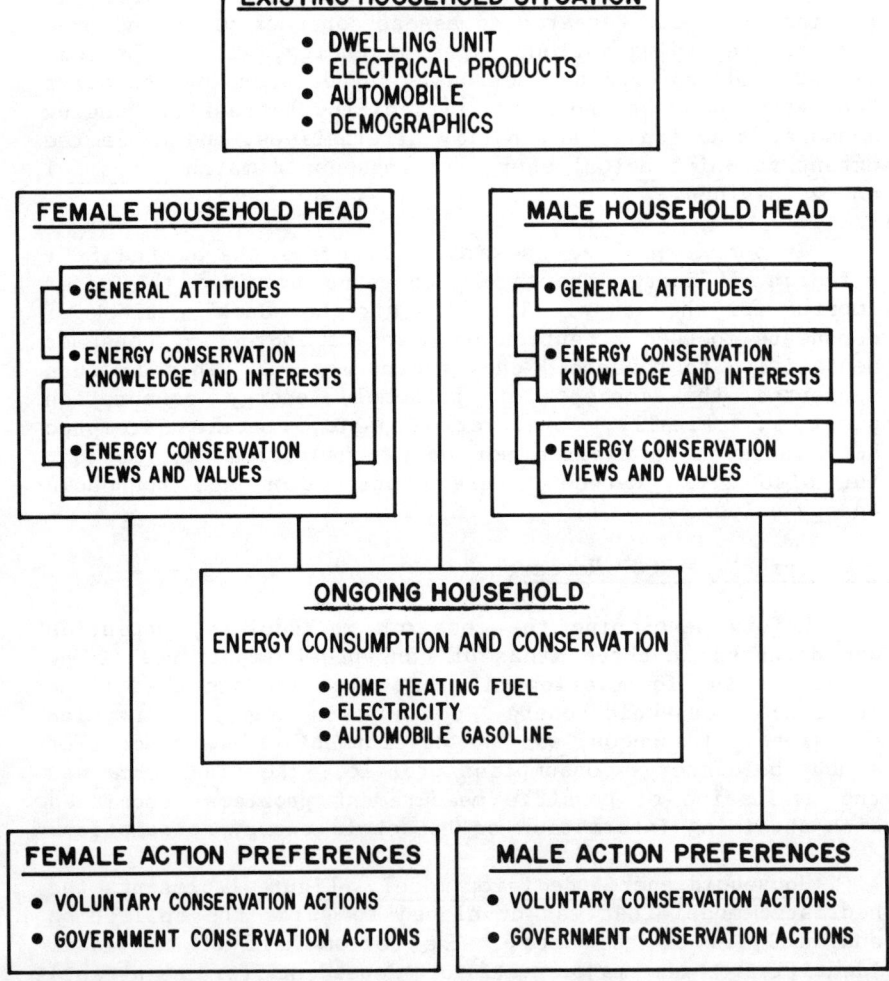

Figure 1
HOUSEHOLD ENERGY DECISION MODEL

other sets are the preferences of females and males for various conservation actions.

The top half of the model identifies three major sets of explanatory (or predictor) variables. One set consists of existing situational factors, such as the dwelling, electrical products, and automobiles owned by the household. The other two sets of variables focus on the energy views and values of each household head.

The model also identifies several anticipated linkages between variable sets. The views and values of the female household head are expected to be related to her conservation action preferences. A similar linkage is expected for the male household head. A more complex and, to some extent, more interesting linkage is the one between the three sets of explanations, variables and the dependent variable based on household behaviors. The energy views and values of both household heads, together with existing situational variables, all have potential for affecting ongoing consumption and conservation. The relative impact of each set of variables was seen as a central concern for ECCP analysis.

Household energy consumption profiles. The second area of conceptual importance was the issue of how to summarize household energy consumption. In a major study done in the United States (Newman and Day 1975) energy consumption had been summarized and discussed in terms of end use, various in-home uses, and various travel uses. Some households might be expected to use a modest amount of energy for each of home heating, appliances, and travel. Others might use realtively little energy for heating and appliances, but a major amount for travel. Being able to recognize differences in consumption patterns is important in understanding the usage and consumption of energy in households and thus was the prime interest of the present study.

DEVELOPMENT OF THE ECCP DATA BASE

This section of the paper describes the ECCP survey conducted during the fall of 1978 and the ECCP research program based on it. Program objectives are discussed first and then survey methodology is summarized.

Research Program Objectives

These were:

- to identify major groupings of households based on energy consumption profiles and energy values;

- to relate these major groupings to situational and demographic factors; and

- to compare the receptivity of the major groupings to alternative energy conservation policy proposals.

These objectives evolved from the background concerns discussed earlier. The first objective was seen as aiding consumer awareness and improving policy evaluation; the second, as helping to understand the determinants of energy consumption; and the third, as asisting in the assessment of alternative policies. Since the major effort of the study was to describe energy consumption and values in the household, the analysis of receptivity to proposals was only preliminary; moreover, to some extent, accomplishment of this third objective depended on attaining the first and second objectives.

Survey Methodology

A national panel of households was the source of the survey data. A panel methodology was adopted because of the need to obtain extensive information from each household (and from both household heads) based on a large national sample. This methodology also produced a satisfactory response rate at an acceptable cost. A national research firm contacted the panel households, none of whose heads had been respondents in surveys of energy research before.

Out of 3,000 Canadian households contacted, data was collected from 2,366, which is a response rate of approximately 79 percent. Several steps were taken prior to administration of the final survey instrument. These included: developing methods to measure energy values; pilot testing of ways to obtain consumption data for home heating and electricity, including back-up information from utilities; and a series of pre-tests of questionnaires leading to the final instrument.

INITIAL FINDINGS AND FUTURE DIRECTIONS

Initial Findings

Presentation is limited to a brief summary of selected findings. Extensive initial analyses, statistics, and descriptions of variables are available in the full report of the present stage of the research (McDougall, Ritchie and Claxton 1979).

The model underlying the research (Figure 1) hypothesized that household energy consumption is a function of demographic (e.g., income) and situational (e.g., climate) variables; also of the views held by household members concerning both energy matters and more general social concerns. Selected aspects of such views will be discussed next.

The importance of energy issues relative to others facing Canadians was assessed by having respondents indicate their views as to the seriousness of five problems (Table 1). Both men and women felt the most serious problem in Canada today was inflation. The cost of energy, to some extent related to inflation, was viewed as second most serious. On the other hand, the energy shortage was seen as least serious of the five problems.

Since their views on energy consumption were expected to be consistent with those on lifestyle, respondents were asked their views on four general topics. These were conservation (not energy specific); work, planning and the future; materialism and "living for today"; and impact of individual efforts on social problems. The expectation was that the views of energy conservationists would be negative on materialism, but positive on the other topics. The strongest view was that on the value of hard work, planning and concern for the future (Table 2). Conversely, respondents were most reluctant to indicate agreement with statements suggesting a materialistic view. Both men and women held somewhat positive views toward conservation, and were neutral regarding the value of individual efforts. Future analyses will seek to confirm the above-mentioned expectation and to link these general views with patterns of energy usages.

A series of 34 energy-related statements were used to assess the components of respondents' views of and knowledge about energy. The statements were grouped according to five

TABLE 1

SERIOUSNESS OF PROBLEMS IN CANADA TODAY

	Mean rating by sex[1]	
Problem:	Women	Men
Inflation	1.23	1.36
Cost of energy	1.48	1.65
Unemployment	1.58	1.74
Pollution	1.96	2.20
Energy shortage	2.10	2.50
Mean issue rating	1.67	1.89

[1] Rating based on a scale of 1 (very serious) to 4 (not at all serious). There were slight variations in the number of respondents answering each item: for women n = 2200 or greater; for men n = 1800 or greater.

TABLE 2

VIEWS ON LIFE STYLE TOPICS AND ENERGY ISSUES

Topics and issues	Mean statement rating by sex[1]		
	Women (n=2283)	Men (n=1861)	Number of statements
General life style topics			
- conservation	.52	.45	4
- work, planning and future orientation	1.41	1.31	6
- materialism and living for today	-.23	-.10	7
- impact of individual efforts on social concerns	.00	.05	3
Energy issues			
- seriousness of energy problem	.71	.67	10
- interest in energy conservation	1.39	1.32	3
- role of individual conservation efforts	.75	.47	11
- conservation through government regulation	.46	.32	7
- role of business in aiding energy conservation	-1.36	-1.32	3

[1] Rating based on a scale of -3 (Definitely Disagree) to +3 (Definitely Agree). Mean statement rating was calculated so that a higher rating indicates a positive view towards each issue. For example, both women (.52) and men (.45) had a positive view towards conservation when the average of the four statements contained in that issue was calculated.

topics: seriousness of the problem; general interest in conservation; and the roles and values of individuals, government, and business in conservation (Table 2). The aggregate data indicate that households tried to push the energy problem off into the future, suggesting that it is not imminent; want to avoid major sacrifices in the present and as long as possible; and tend to view others, such as business, as being more responsible than consumers for the problem and, hence, under greater obligation to conserve. Interestingly, there was more agreement with indicators of general interest in energy than with specific energy activities.

Familiarity with information about energy consumption was evaluated in two ways. First, respondents were asked whether they knew a series of energy facts; second, their knowledge was tested through a series of true-false questions and a set of questions requiring energy savings estimates. Although respondents stated a relatively high level of awareness of energy facts (not reported here) energy savings estimates (Table 3) suggested that they were possibly less informed than they would like to imply. Of the seven estimates aggregated separately for male and female respondents, only one was "correct." Correct answers were supplied by the federal department of Consumer and Corporate Affairs based on a review of energy savings (Cullen 1978).

Assessment of the willingness of householders to voluntarily conserve energy was made by asking them what they would be willing to do in the future. They indicated they would be willing to lower thermostats (Table 4) on the average to approximately 66.9°F; this would represent a net reduction of only 3°, since current temperature settings are reported to range from 69°F to 70°F. They also indicated willingness to cut back annual mileage driven by 1,600 miles, by reducing vacation and leisure travel but not changing mileage devoted to shopping or commuting to work. (Table 5).

These results for conservation of home heating and gasoline suggest that Canadian households are willing to adopt only minor conservation behaviors. From a conserver society viewpoint it is clear that there is no groundswell of support for major changes in lifestyle. Rather the "I'm all right, Jack" syndrome described earlier appears to be the current philosophy for the majority of Canadian households.

TABLE 3

CONSUMERS' ENERGY KNOWLEDGE BY SEX
(ENERGY SAVINGS ESTIMATES)

Question (abridged) : How much do you think could be saved in each of the following situations:	Modal Estimate[1] (% Savings)		Percentage of sample that gave an estimate	
	Women	Men	Women	Men
For each Fahrenheit degree below 68°F you set your thermostat at, your fuel saving is about what percent ?	5	5	36.6	42.9
Using radial tires instead of ordinary tires can mean a fuel saving of up to what percent ?	10	5	24.8	47.4
A frost-free refrigerator rather than a manual defrost refrigerator increases electricity usage by about what percent ?	10	10	47.3	46.3
Getting your furnace checked and cleaned twice a year can save you up to what percent ?	10	10	47.4	49.6
Adding storm windows and doors, weatherstripping and caulking can result in a fuel saving of up to what percent ?	20	20	67.5	63.2
A major furnace modification (retrofitting) can result in a fuel saving of up to what percent ?	20	10	23.3	30.0
Driving at 55 mph instead of 70 mph can result in a fuel saving of what percent ?	10	10	62.8	66.0

[1] The real impact of each conservation action is estimated as follows: each degree below 68°, 2 1/2% ; radial tires, 10% ; manual vs. frost-free, 50% ; furnace maintenance, 20% ; storm windows and caulking, 30% ; furnace retrofitting, 30% ; 55 vs. 70 mph, 20% (Cullen 1978).

TABLE 4

VOLUNTARY CONSERVATION EFFORTS
(HOME HEATING)[1]

Temperature range of cutback	Percentage of respondents by sex[2] for each cutback level	
	Women	Men
under 60°F	1.1	1.3
60°F to 63°F	7.1	8.1
64°F to 66°F	30.0	31.4
67°F to 69°F	45.4	46.1
70°F to 72°F	15.8	12.1
over 72°F	0.6	1.0

[1] Results based on following question (abridged): <u>Suppose an energy shortage occurred in Canada this winter</u>, and Canadians were asked to cut back the temperature in their homes. What temperature would you be willing to keep your home at <u>during the day</u> when there are <u>people at home</u>?

[2] Based on 2,283 women and 1,861 men respondents.

TABLE 5

VOLUNTARY CONSERVATION EFFORTS
(AUTOMOBILE)

Mileage range of cutback[2]	Percentage of respondents by sex for each cutback range[1]	
	Women	Men
Could not cut back	23.0	17.2
Cut back about 1,000 miles a year	34.3	26.9
Cut back between 1,000 and 2,000 miles	20.6	21.5
Cut back between 2,000 and 3,000 miles	9.9	14.5
Cut back between 3,000 and 4,000 miles	4.6	7.5
Cut back over 4,000 miles a year	7.6	12.4

Type of activity which would be cut back[3]	Order of cutback	
	Women	Men
Commuting to work/school	5	5
Shopping trips	4	4
Long vacation trips (500 or more miles from home)	1	1
Short vacation trips (100 to 500 miles from home)	2	2
Recreation/leisure/social trips (visiting friends, out for a drive, going to a show, etc.)	3	3

[1] Based on 2040 women and 1761 men respondents.

[2] Based on this mileage cutback question (abridged): <u>Suppose</u> there was a disruption in our oil supplies, which meant that rationing of gasoline was necessary. How much could your household cut back on the number of miles driven each year?

[3] Based on this activity cutback question (abridged): <u>Suppose</u> there was a disruption in our oil supplies, which meant that every household had to cut back on driving. Which one of these five would your household cut back FIRST? SECOND? THIRD? FOURTH? FIFTH?

Future Directions

The overview presented here of energy consumption and conservation in Canadian households, which is based on aggregate statistics, will soon be followed by the results of analysis, now underway, on differing energy pattterns from household to household.

As a forecast of what lies ahead in ECCP research in the longer term, it is useful to return to the consideration of conservation policy selection. Policy selection was described as requiring (1) a determination of potential policy payoffs and (2) an assessment of the extent to which these payoffs will likely be achieved. This might be accomplished by developing a policy impact model using computer simulation. If this model included both technical energy savings and behavioral reactions, policy makers could use it to answer questions such as: what is the net energy savings from a particular policy, and which consumers will be affected?

Useful as such a model would be in simplifying policy decisions, ECCP research serves a larger purpose. It is to gradually piece together behavioral information about energy consumption so that policy makers can better understand the proportion of potential payoff that would likely accrue to various conservation alternatives. While others are developing a matrix of potential policy payoffs, ECCP research is building the corresponding behavioral understanding for the analysis of policy impacts.

Based on our interpretation of the initial findings of this study, it appears that behavioral change policies will be strongly resisted by consumers until energy concerns become more significant to them. Such increased concern may be forced upon consumers by environmental events which impose substantially lower supplies of high cost energy with resultant sudden disruptions in lifestyles. Hopefully such a scenario can be averted by formulation and implementation of energy management programs which succeed in developing a national awareness of the need to move towards the conserver society in an orderly yet determined fashion.

REFERENCES

Cullen, Carman (1978), *The Potential for Energy Conservation in the Residential Sector*, Consumer & Corporate Affairs Canada, Ottawa, Ontario.

EMR (1977), *Energy Conservation in Canada: Programs and Perspectives*, Energy Mines and Resources Canada, Report EP77-7, Ottawa, Canada.

EMR (1978), *Energy Future for Canadians*, Energy Mines and Resources Canada, Report EP78-2, Ottawa, Canada.

Evans, John L., J.R. Brent Ritchie and Gordon H.G. McDougall (1979), "Energy Use and Consumer Behavior: A Framework for Analysis and Policy Formulation", *Journal of Business Administration* (forthcoming).

McDougall, Gordon H.G. and Gerald Keller (1979), "The Energy Issue: A Four Year Canadian Investigation of Attitudes and Behaviors", *Proceedings of the American Institute for the Decision Sciences*.

McDougall, Gordon H.G., J.R. Brent Ritchie and John D. Claxton (1979), *Energy Consumption and Conservation Patterns in Canadian Households: An Overview and Aggregate Statistics*, Consumer and Corporate Affairs, Canada, Ottawa, Ontario.

Newman, Dorothy K, and Dawn Day (1975), *The American Energy Consumer*, Cambridge, Mass.: Ballinger Publishing Company.

Shapiro, Stanley J. (1978), "Marketing in a Conserver Society", *Business Horizons*, (April), 3-13.

CONSUMER ENERGY CONSERVATION RESEARCH ACTIVITY IN CANADA

L.G. McCabe, Carman W. Cullen, Consumer Research and Evaluation Branch, Consumer and Corporate Affairs Canada, Hull, Quebec.

INTRODUCTION

In the relatively brief period following the OPEC oil embargo of 1973, energy research has come to occupy an increasingly important position among government priorities. The Canadian government, in response to these shifting objectives, has undertaken an extensive energy research effort directed at achieving energy self-reliance in the next decade. Although Canada's research addresses both the supply and demand dimensions of the energy problem, this paper will focus on demand solutions -- energy conservation research.

Canada's energy research and development activity is divided into six tasks, each of which is coordinated by a designated government agency. The six tasks and their coordinating agencies are listed in **Table 1**.

TABLE 1

THE SIX TASKS OF CANADA'S FEDERAL ENERGY R&D ACTIVITY

Task	Coordinating Agency
1 Conservation	Energy, Mines and Resources Canada
2 Fossil Fuels	Energy, Mines and Resources Canada
3 Nuclear Energy	Atomic Energy of Canada Limited
4 Renewable Resources	National Research Council
5 Energy Transmission & Transportation	Transport Canada
6 Coordination	Interdepartmental Panel on Energy R&D

Each of the tasks of Canada's energy research and development activity is divided into several programs which are managed by selected government agencies. Task 1, Conservation, is organized into the 10 functional programs listed in **Table 2**.

TABLE 2

THE 10 PROGRAMS OF TASK 1 - CONSERVATION

<u>Program</u>   <u>Managing Agency</u>

1.1 Energy Efficiency in Buildings   National Research
     - addresses energy conservation   Council
       R&D in residential, commercial
       and institutional buildings.
     - focuses on the building
       envelope, mechanical and
       electrical systems, internal
       environment, building
       orientation and system
       performance.

1.2 Energy Efficiency in the   Transport Canada
     Transportation System
     - addresses energy conservation
       in passenger and freight
       transportation.
     - focuses on technical improvements
       to various modes of transportation
       plus an examination of energy
       and travel substitution.

1.3 Energy Efficiency in the Food   Agriculture Canada
     Supply System
     - addresses energy conservation
       in farm production, processing,
       transportation, distribution
       and home preparation and
       storage.
     - focuses on the farm and the
       food processing industry.

1.4 Thermal Waste as an Energy Source   Energy, Mines and
     - addresses the utilization of   Resources Canada
       waste heat as an energy source.
     - focuses on the waste heat
       from thermal generation of
       electricity.

111

TABLE 2 (Cont'd)

Program	Managing Agency
1.5 Municipal and Industrial Waste Reclamation - addresses energy conservation benefits achievable through waste recovery. - focuses on combustion, pyrolysis, bioconversion and industrial waste.	Environment Canada
1.6 Energy Efficiency in the Burning of Oil, Gas and Coal - addresses the achievement of energy savings through improved energy efficiency in the burning of various fuels. - focuses on industrial combustion processes, and domestic or small scale applications.	Energy, Mines and Resources Canada
1.7 Industrial Processes - addresses the energy usage of industry, including energy supply industries and non-energy uses. - focuses on industrial energy research and development and the development of new industrial processes.	Industry, Trade and Commerce Canada
1.8 Energy Conversion and Storage - addresses the development of advanced technologies in conversion, storage and energy carriers. - focuses on problems associated with energy conversion, energy storage, and the production, transmission, storage and utilization of hydrogen systems.	National Research Council

TABLE 2 (Cont'd)

Program	Managing Agency

1.9 Community Energy Systems
 - addresses the potential for energy conservation in community-based systems such as district heating.

Central Mortgage and Housing Corporation; Energy, Mines and Resources Canada

1.10 Consumer Products and Lifestyles
 - addresses energy consumption and energy conservation in the consumer sector.
 - focuses on the purchase and use of all consumer products.

Consumer and Corporate Affairs Canada

As can be seen from the program titles and research descriptions of Table 2, the majority of the conservation research is directed towards supply-oriented technology and, accordingly, at commercial, industrial and government targets. This is in accordance with the research priorities that were established, and that are being continuously reviewed by the Interdepartmental Panel on Energy Research and Development. However, the importance of consumer energy consumption and conservation has not been ignored by the Panel. Program 1.10, Consumer Products and Lifestyles, was established in April 1978 to perform just this kind of research and the Consumer Research and Evaluation Branch (CREB) of Consumer and Corporate Affairs Canada (CCAC) was designated as the managing agency. CREB is responsible for carrying out the bulk of consumer behaviour research within the Canadian Federal Government and is, accordingly, the primary consumer energy conservation research agency in Canada.

CREB'S CONSUMER ENERGY CONSERVATION RESEARCH PROGRAM

The focus of Program 1.10 is on the energy intensity of consumer lifestyles and products. Research is being carried out to develop effective and efficient consumer energy conservation policies which will contribute to reducing the growth rate of overall energy demand.

Too often, as noted by Mazis and McNeill (1978) and Wilkie and Gardner (1974), consumer public policy has been based on little or no consumer research. Furthermore, a great deal of energy research has been conducted without devoting much thought to relating the research to public policy. The Consumer Research and Evaluation Branch of CCAC has developed a policy formulation framework that imparts a policy orientation to energy research. Without such an orientation, it is easy to lose sight of the ultimate purpose of research and evaluation activities. Moreover, without supportive research, policies may more easily become arbitrary and inconsistent. The framework, described briefly in this paper, is explained in detail in Evans, McDougall and Ritchie (1979).

The framework is a behaviourally based process, consisting of six stages: (1) Problem Identification and Analysis, (2) Policy Definition, (3) Impact Analysis and Policy Selection, (4) Program Development, (5) Program Implementation and (6) Program Evaluation and Modification.

CREB's energy research consolidates this framework into three stages: Problems, Policies and Programs.

The first stage -- identification and analysis of of problems -- consists of conducting baseline studies or foundation research to determine the nature and extent of energy-related problems in the consumer sector. The studies assess consumers' attitudes, interests, opinions, knowledge and behaviours with respect to energy. They identify the critical characteristics of the problem, estimate their magnitude and specify the nature of relationships between the major variables.

Foundation studies must contain an appropriate blend of the general and the specific. The former is necessary to obtain a comprehensive understanding of the problem; the latter, to isolate and define the principal dimensions of the problem.

The second stage of the framework -- policy definition, analysis and selection -- deals with specific problems and includes: (1) specifying policy objectives, (2) defining policy content foci, targets and types and (3) assessing the probable impact of policy alternatives.

From CREB's energy research flow two general policy objectives: to encourage energy conserving behaviour by consumers and to encourage the production of energy-efficient consumer products.

Policy foci may be organized into four major groups. The first is policy intervention, which may impact on the availability of the product or service, the decision used to select it, or the nature and extent of product use after purchase. The second group, expanding on the first, includes product or service type, location, time, quantity, recipient and end purpose. The third group of policy foci is the form of energy under consideration. Essentially this distinguishes between renewable and non-renewable energy sources. The fourth group is the kind of consumption activity, namely, whether it is home-related, work-related or leisure-related.

Policy targets refer to the marketplace actor(s) toward which the policy is directed. They include, singly or in combination, ultimate consumers, intermediate consumers, distributors, producers and energy suppliers.

Policy type, the final component of policy content, may be thought of as a 2 x 2 matrix with one dimension being financial or non-financial and the second being persuasive or mandatory. The result is four distinct types of policy: persuasive financial policies such as incentives; persuasive non-financial policies such as labelling; mandatory financial policy such as excise taxes and mandatory non-financial policies such as rationing.

Once the content of policies has been defined, their potential impact may be assessed and the appropriate policy selected. The policy selection will be made according to three main criteria: the size and nature of the energy savings, the impact on consumers, and the enforcibility of the policy.

The third stage of the Policy Formulation Framework is the development, implementation and evaluation of energy conservation programs. Clearly, the step from theoretical policy analysis to practical implementation of policies through programs is crucial to the success of an energy conservation effort. However, this step is hindered by a myriad of intervening variables. CCAC's policy-oriented research facilitates this transfer from the theoretical to the practical. Policy and Program evaluation research invariably uncovers additional aspects of the problem that, in turn, identify more effective or efficient means of achieving specified policy objectives.

PROBLEMS

Several of CREB's energy research projects are foundation studies that focus on the first stage of the policy formulation framework -- problem identification and analysis. Their main function is to provide certain baseline data and fundamental analyses.

The energy conservation research being conducted in the Problem section is typified by Study 1.10.1-1, A Taxonomy of

Consumer Energy Use Lifestyles. This study represents the first Canadian effort to measure the relative size and the economic, social and other characteristics of major groups of consumers as categorized by energy conservation attitudes and energy consumption patterns. A nationwide consumer survey was conducted to measure value systems and stated behaviour regarding energy conservation. Actual energy consumption data, with the consent of the subjects, was collected through the cooperation of the energy suppliers. Factor analysis and related techniques are being used to separate respondents into groups based on their attitudes/behaviour and their propensity towards energy conservation.

Study 1.10.1-2, Analysis of the Energy Situation Attitudes Survey, is an investigation and revision of an annual (since 1975) study of the Canadian public's attitudes toward the energy situation.

Study 1.10.1-4, Consumer Energy Conservation Bibliography, is an annotated bibliography of the relevant literature dealing with consumer attitudes, behavioural intentions and behaviour in respect to energy.

Study 1.10.1-5, Conservation Potential within Consumer Leisure and Recreational Activities, is an analysis of the potential for energy conservation in consumer leisure and recreational activities.

Study 1.10.1-6, Consumer Products and Lifestyles Potential Energy Savings Matrix, is an effort to develop and maintain a thorough, well-documented quantitative assessment of the potential for consumer energy conservation in the residential sector.

Study 1.10.1-7, Overview Paper on Life Cycle Costing, is a baseline study on the feasibility of using Life Cycle Costing in residential energy conservation programs.

Study 1.10.1-9, Overview Topic Paper on the Rand Experiments, is a foundation investigation of the potential for transferring the Rand studies on "time-of-day" pricing to Canada.

POLICIES

Policy definition, impact analysis and policy selection are critical since during these stages key recommendations will be made. While the task of specifying the overall policy objectives is relatively easy, determining appropriate policy content and assessing the potential impact of policy alternatives on an "a priori" basis are both most important and most difficult.

Study 1.10.2-1, Decision-Making in the Purchase of Heating Equipment and Major Appliances for New Housing and Rental Accommodations, is a typical "policy" study. The majority of heating equipment and major appliances in consumers' residences are purchased by intermediaries and consumers have little direct input into the purchase decision process. It is thus important to study the decision-making process of these intermediaries and assess the potential for, and ways and means of increasing the value of energy use as a purchase criteria. An analysis of purchases which are "imposed" and "non-imposed" for each type of major appliance and heating equipment used in residential buildings has been performed. The relative influence of different parties (architect, landlord, construction engineer, building manager, subcontractor) in the purchase decision process and the relevance of the energy usage have been investigated. Finally an assessment has been made of the likely impact of alternative policy approaches on raising the salience of energy usage considerations in "imposed choice" purchase decisions.

Study 1.10.2-2, Consumer Products Packaging Conservation, is an investigation of the extent to which consumers prefer lightly packaged to "over-packaged" consumer goods.

Study 1.10.2-3, Point-of-Purchase Energy Information Disclosure and Consumer Choice Behaviour, is an analysis of the role of energy information at the point of sale in the purchase of major appliances.

Study 1.10.2-4, Overview Topic Paper on Mass Media Energy Conservation Communications Policy, examines the potential for utilizing information diffusion strategies to increase consumer energy conservation efforts.

Study 1.10.2-5, Microeconomic Energy Conservation Policy Analysis, is an inventory and analysis of microeconomic energy conservation policy alternatives.

Study 1.10.2-6, Overview Topic Paper on Energy Use Feedback and Consumer Behaviour, examines the use of energy consumption information feedback to modify energy consumption.

Study 1.10.2-7, An Evaluation of Selected Consumer Energy Conservation Policies from a Government, Business and Consumer Perspective, concentrates on mandatory non-financial policy alternatives available to policymakers.

PROGRAMS

Stages four, five and six of the Policy Formulation Framework are, respectively, the development, implementation and evaluation of consumer energy conservation programs. The role of research in four and five is to ensure that the results of policy analysis research results are accurately transformed into program operations. In stage six, research is necessary to accurately measure the efficiency and effectiveness of policies and programs.

Another type of research that falls into this category is the demonstration project. These action research studies are based on existing theoretical and empirical knowledge and involve the scientific investigation of certain products, program concepts and/or behavioural modification techniques.

Study 1.10.3-1, ENERGUIDE Evaluation, is an extensive appraisal of Canada's energy consumption labelling scheme for appliances. The evaluation will: (1) investigate and measure changes in consumer, retailer and manufacturer/industry performance attributable to the program, (2) perform a comprehensive and rigourous cost-benefit analysis of the program, and (3) identify ways and means of improving the program content and administration.

Study 1.10.3-3, Community Energy Conservation Through Citizen Participation, has two main goals: (1) to examine the possibility of generating energy conserving behaviour in communities through citizen participation and involvement, (2) to develop a model of the process of achieving citizen participation and initiative that may be transferred to other communities. The study will take place in three test communities. Quantitative and qualitative data will be collected and will be compared with historical data plus data from three comparison communities.

Study 1.10.3-4, Energy Cost Indicator Pilot Project, is an extension of the energy-use feedback and consumer behaviour study (1.10.2-6). The U.S. Department of Energy has developed an accurate energy cost indicator (ECI) for use in residential settings. The ECI provides information on electricity and natural gas consumption, converted to dollars and cents, for the consumer at any point in time plus a cumulative feature that allows the consumer to determine the cost of the energy he has consumed so far in the month and in the previous 24 hours. This study is a joint program with the U.S. Department of Energy, the Canadian Electrical Association and nine utilities in six North American cities (Boston, Dallas, Minneapolis, Montreal, San Francisco and Vancouver). The study will attempt to measure the impact of the ECIs on energy consumption in 100 residences in each city by measuring: (1) homeowners' consumption of electricity and/or natural gas over a one year period, (2) homeowners' knowledge and attitudes toward energy and resource conservation, (3) homeowners' consumption of other energy sources.

CONCLUSION

This paper has been devoted to a brief sketch of energy conservation research in Canada. The place of this research within the Federal Energy Research and Development Activity has been defined. The role of the research in policy development and in the structuring of the program has been reviewed.

The issue of marketing the results of the research has not been discussed, nor has such marketing been made an operational task as yet, since the results are only now beginning to be reported. However, it is clear that the potential clientele of the program exist outside Consumer and Corporate Affairs Canada and outside the federal government. For certain studies, e.g. the Energy Cost Indicator Pilot Project, manufacturers of products and utilities supplying energy to households are the obvious clients. Indeed, they are already in active contact with CCAC at the present time. However, for studies whose research applications are not so obvious or are more general in nature, a more active approach must be taken. To that end, a well planned and effective communications strategy is currently being developed so that other federal departments and agencies, other levels of government and all sectors of the business community may learn of this research and incorporate it in their decision making.

REFERENCES

Evans, John L., Gordon H.G. McDougall and J.R. Brent Ritchie (1979), "Energy Use and Consumer Behaviour - A Framework for Analysis and Policy Formulation," forthcoming in Journal of Business Administration.

Mazis, Michael and Dennis McNeill (1978), "The Use of Marketing Research in FTC Decision Making", in Research Frontiers in Marketing: Dialogues and Directions, Subhash Jain, ed., Chicago: American Marketing Association.

Wilkie, William L. and David M. Gardner (1974), "The Role of Marketing Research in Public Policy Decision Making," Journal of Marketing, 38 (January), 38-47.

GOVERNMENT AND THE ENERGY CONSCIOUS CONSUMER:
THE APPLIANCE ENERGY LABELING PROGRAM

Kenneth L. Bernhardt, Federal Trade
Commission and Georgia State University[1]

INTRODUCTION

The 1979 gasoline "crunch" stressed once again the importance of adopting a national energy program. Although there are many different perceptions of what elements should be included in such a program, most would agree that energy conservation measures should play a key role. The purpose of this paper is to present one example of how marketing concepts and practices can be applied by the government to motivate and facilitate energy conservation by consumers.

Estimates by the Department of Energy indicate that approximately one-fourth of the energy consumed in the United States occurs in residences. Because appliances represent a significant part of such consumption, Congress, as part of the Energy Policy and Conservation Act (EPCA 1975) passed in December 1975, established two programs to reduce the amount of energy consumed by household appliances.

The Act, as amended by the National Energy Conservation Policy Act (NECPA 1978), requires (a) the Federal Trade Commission (FTC) to mandate labels for appliances indicating their energy consumption, and (b) the Department of Energy (DOE) to develop efficiency improvement targets. Both labeling and targets must be based on test procedures determined by DOE.

PROPOSED RULE

In August 1979, the FTC approved in substance a rule requiring a number of major home appliance manufacturers to place energy labels on appliances in a number of different categories. A final rule is expected to be passed by the Commission in late

---

[1] The views expressed in this paper are the author's and do not represent the views of the Federal Trade Commission or any individual Commissioner. The author wishes to acknowledge the substantial assistance of Andrew I. Wolf, Lucerne D. Winfrey and Kent C. Hoverton, Attorneys in the Division of Energy and Product Information, Bureau of Consumer Protection, Federal Trade Commission.

September, 1979. The rest of this paper describes the proposed program, as of August, 1979. The reader should note that changes may be made in the proposed rule and, consequently, parts of this paper may be rendered obsolete. However, the author anticipates only minor changes, if any, and they should not affect the principal description of the program set forth here.

The EPCA lists 13 categories of appliances to be labeled. They are:

(1) Refrigerators and refrigerator-freezers
(2) Freezers
(3) Dishwashers
(4) Clothes dryers
(5) Water heaters
(6) Room air conditioners
(7) Home heating equipment, not including furnaces
(8) Television sets
(9) Kitchen ranges and ovens
(10) Clothes washers
(11) Humidifiers and dehumidifiers
(12) Central air conditioners
(13) Furnaces

In addition, the Act included a forteenth category to allow the Administrator of the Federal Energy Administration (now DOE) to add products if they have an average annual per household energy consumption of at least 100 kilowatt-hours. The FTC is required to mandate labels for the appliances unless (a) DOE is unable to develop test procedures, (b) the labeling would be technically or economically infeasible, or (c) the labels would be unlikely to assist consumers.

The recommended Rule (FTC 1979) would require labels for only seven of the thirteen appliances considered. During the rulemaking proceedings it was determined that, regardless of model or manufacturer, all electric home heating equipment other than furnaces will provide about the same amount of heat and will cost about the same to operate. Vented home heating equipment (gas, oil and propane heaters) other than furnaces is a rapidly dying industry with most sales being replacement sales to the poor and elderly. The FTC staff concluded that labels for electric products were unlikely to assist consumers, and that for vented products, labels were economically infeasible, given (a) the small variation in energy consumption among the alternatives, (b) the decaying nature of this industry which has little economic incentive for new entrants into the market, and (c) the cost of the labels themselves.

Television sets are to be excluded for several reasons. Sets typically use little energy, with the cost of operating a second or third set as low as one dollar or less per year. Television usage varies considerably from household to household, making it difficult to determine an average annual energy cost that is meaningful. The cost variation among all models -- regardless of screen size--is low, perhaps six dollars per year. Finally, a strong incentive already exists for manufacturers to lower energy consumption because lower energy usage allows for lower operating temperatures and thereby increases the reliability of the sets.

Kitchen ranges and ovens, clothes dryers, and humidifiers and dehumidifiers have been excluded from the recommended rule. For each of these appliances, the variation in energy cost from the lowest to the highest cost unit is approximately six dollars or less per year for the average household. It is unlikely that differences of that magnitude would be helpful to consumers or worth the cost associated with requiring the labels. Also these appliances have variable useage characteristics which limit the utility of any uniform type of disclosure on a label. These characteristics are detailed in the FTC Staff Report (1979).

Label Formats

Appliance energy labels must provide accurate and relevant information if the consumer is to make effective use of the information when buying an appliance. EPCA requires that two pieces of information must appear on each appliance label: **the estimated annual operating cost and a range of estimated** annual operating costs for comparable products. Under certain circumstances the FTC can require that the label contain a different measure of energy consumption, such as an energy efficiency ratio. Any alternative measure must be capable of being determined in accordance with DOE testing procedures.

In addition, the labels must contain three other disclosures. The first is a general qualification similar to what is mandated by the EPA Fuel Economy Guide: "Your cost will vary depending on your local energy rate and how you use this product. Ask your local utility or salesperson for the energy rate (cost per KWH or BTU) in your area" (this qualification varies somewhat depending on the appliance). The second is information about how the average cost figure was obtained, for example, indicating what kilowatt hour cost of electricity was used to determine the average energy consumption for refrigerators.

The third disclosure is a table or grid showing how the energy cost can vary with a wide range of utility rates, and, when applicable with different usage patterns. This information allows consumers to determine more easily the actual energy costs they would incur when using the appliance.

As part of the test procedures, DOE determined a representative use cycle for each product. For example, for dishwashers, clothes washers, and clothes dryers, DOE declared the average usage to be eight loads per week or 416 per year. Refrigerators, refrigerator-freezers ahd water heaters all reflect a single amount of usage, based on an assumption of consistent daily consumption of energy for most households.

The interpretation grid concept allows consumers whose usage differs from the average to estimate their annual energy cost. This capability is important. Consider a dishwasher used for two loads per week in a low energy cost area (2 cents per kilowatt hour and assuming an electric water heater) compared to one used for twelve loads per week in a high cost area (12 cents per kilowatt hour). The difference in annual cost of operating the dishwashers would be $270 ($8 versus $278).

The ranges of energy cost per year mandated on the label are based on functional comparability of the appliances rather than on their design characteristics. For example, refrigerator-freezers of about the same size which store about the same amount of food can be compared, without regard to whether the design is top-mounted or side-by-side or whether or not the freezer has an automatic defrost. All heating and cooling equipment is compared on the basis of output (ability to heat or cool about the same amount of space).

Figure 1 contains a sample label for a refrigerator-freezer. At the top left of the label all the pertinent information concerning the make, model number, capacity and type of defrost is provided. Underneath the "Energyguide" headline, the national average energy rate that was used to calculate various average cost figures is disclosed, together with the specifications used to define comparable models. Below that, in large bold type, the average annual energy cost figure is presented along with, in smaller bold type, the corresponding figures for the models with the highest and lowest energy cost. An arrow is placed on the line connecting these figures in order to indicate where on the continuum the particular model fits (not far from the middle of the range in this example).

FIGURE 1

SAMPLE LABEL FOR REFRIGERATOR-FREEZER

(Name of Corporation)
Refrigerator-Freezer
Model(s) AH503, AH504, AH507
Capacity: 23 Cubic Feet
Type of Defrost: Full Automatic

Estimates on the scale are based on a national average electric rate of 4.1¢ per kilowatt hour.

Only models with 22.5 to 24.4 cubic feet are compared in the scale.

Model with lowest energy cost
$68

$91
THIS ▼ MODEL
Estimated yearly energy cost

Model with highest energy cost
$132

This energy cost is based on U.S. Government standard tests.

How much will this model cost you to run yearly?

		Yearly cost
		Yearly $ cost shown below
Cost per kilowatt hour	2¢	$44
	4¢	$88
	6¢	$132
	8¢	$176
	10¢	$220
	12¢	$264

Ask your salesperson or local utility for the energy rate (cost per kilowatt hour) in your area. Your cost will vary depending on your local energy rate.

Important

Removal of this label before consumer purchase is a violation of federal law (42 U.S.C. 6302).

(Part No. 371026)

The bottom half of the label presents the grid, which in this case only contains alternative energy costs for different energy cost areas. The consumer is told to ask the salesperson or contact the local utility to determine the cost per kilowatt hour for his or her area. Finally, the balel discloses that the cost to the consumer will vary depending on the local rates, and it informs the retailer that removal of the label is a violation of federal law.

The additional complexity associated with the label for dishwashers is shown in Figure 2. Here separate grids must be included for situations where electric and gas water heaters are used because of the substantial impact on the amount of energy used. As pointed out above, the actual amount of energy consumed can vary substantially from the average, and so the grids allow consumers to more accurately determine the costs for their own situation. This variation was a source of controversy during the public hearings held as part of the rulemaking process, and will be discussed below.

ANNUAL ENERGY COST VERSUS ENERGY EFFICIENCY RATING

Although most industry and consumer witnesses during the hearings were supportive of the appliance energy labeling program (<u>Advertising Age</u> 1978 and <u>FTC News Summary</u> 1979), there were criticisms of the selected measure of energy consumption (<u>Consumers Reports</u> 1979 and FTC 1979, 40-46). Some believe that consumers will use the average figures not only as a comparative figure to evaluate alternative appliances, but also will take the figures to be accurate indications of the actual costs they will incur, regardless of their usage patterns or utility rates.

Although Congress was probably aware of this potential problem, it decided that the benefits of a single average cost figure so outweigh any drawbacks that the annual cost for most covered products should be mandated. These benefits might include a greater understanding of costs; the ability of dollar costs to provide greater motivation than alternative measures of energy conservation; the uniformity of disclosure across product categories; the ability to make interfuel comparisons; and the possibility of eventually requiring disclosures of life cycle costs.

The main benefit of the energy efficiency ratio for climate control equipment only is the ability to express energy consumption in comparative terms, unlike dollar cost disclosures, which may sometimes be accepted unquestioningly

FIGURE 2

SAMPLE LABEL FOR DISHWASHER

(Name of Corporation)

Dishwasher
Model(s) MR328, XL12, NA83
Capacity: Standard

Estimates on the scale are based on a national average electric rate of 4.1¢ per kilowatt hour and a natural gas rate of 28¢ per therm.

Only standard size dishwashers are used in the scale.

Electric Water Heater

Model with lowest energy cost $50

$60

Model with highest energy cost $84

▼ THIS MODEL

Estimated yearly energy cost

Gas Water Heater

Model with lowest energy cost $19

$27

Model with highest energy cost $42

▼ THIS MODEL

Estimated yearly energy cost

This energy cost is based on U.S. Government standard tests.

How much will this model cost you to run yearly?

with an electric water heater

Loads of dishes per week		2	4	6	8	12
		Yearly $ cost shown below.				
Cost per kilowatt hour	2¢	$8	$15	$23	$31	$47
	4¢	$15	$31	$46	$62	$92
	6¢	$23	$46	$69	$92	$139
	8¢	$31	$62	$92	$123	$189
	10¢	$39	$77	$116	$154	$231
	12¢	$47	$92	$139	$185	$278

with a gas water heater

Loads of dishes per week		2	4	6	8	12
		Yearly $ cost shown below				
Cost per therm (100 cubic feet)	10¢	$2	$5	$7	$9	$14
	20¢	$5	$11	$16	$22	$33
	30¢	$7	$14	$21	$27	$41
	40¢	$9	$19	$28	$36	$55
	50¢	$12	$23	$35	$45	$68
	60¢	$19	$28	$42	$54	$82

Ask your salesperson or local utility for the energy rate (cost per kilowatt hour or therm) in your area, and for the estimated costs if you have a propane or oil water heater.

Important

Removal of this label before consumer purchase is a violation of federal law (42 U.S.C. 6302).

(Part No. 73906)

by consumers. The purpose of the grid is to demonstrate to consumers that the average cost can vary (beyond the disclaimer on the label) depending on usage and rates.

Climate control equipment is treated differently from other appliances covered in the proposed rule. Refrigerator-freezers, clothes washers, and the other products for which cost disclosures are required, are free-standing products which function upon demand of the consumer. Air conditioners and furnaces are climate sensitive, operating differently in different geographical locations in order to maintain a predetermined temperature in summer and winter. For these products, it was decided, given the unpredictable number of hours of operation which would accurately reflect consumer usage patterns, that energy efficiency ratings would be more beneficial to consumers. An example of this type of label is presented in Figure 3.

To assist in decisions as to the type and format of disclosure to mandate, several consumer research studies were conducted. These are described in the next section of this paper.

CONSUMER RESEARCH

The FTC staff decided to conduct consumer research on energy labeling for several reasons. First, knowledge of energy costs is important to the consumer and to the nation. Second, the prototype labels are the first ones for which the FTC has specified the form as well as the content. The research was designed to evaluate the overall ability of the labels to attract consumers and to communicate effectively. Also, the research was intended to help ascertain which of several alternative formats would be most successful in communicating energy consumption information.

In formulating the original design and wording of the labels, the FTC staff worked closely with a prominent language expert, a leading design firm and the National Bureau of Standards. The combination of experts produced several label formats which presented some rather complex technical information in sufficiently simple language to achieve a high score ("fairly easy") on a readability test.

The second stage of the research consisted of six sessions of focus group interviews, conducted in Princeton, Atlanta and Los Angeles. The focus groups provided general guidance on how consumers purchase appliances, how salient energy information is to them when they shop and how they express ideas

FIGURE 3

SAMPLE LABEL FOR ROOM AIR CONDITIONER

(Name of Corporation)
Room Air Conditioner
Model(s) SA 714, SA 718
Capacity: 10,000 BTU/hr

ENERGYGUIDE

Models with the most efficient energy rating number use less energy and cost less to operate.

Models with 7,700 to 10,199 BTU's cool about the same space.

7.3

Least efficient model
3.4
▼

THIS MODEL ▼

Most efficient model
8.5
▼

Energy Efficiency Rating (EER)

This energy rating is based on U.S. Government standard tests.

How much will this model cost you to run yearly?

Yearly hours of use		250	750	1000	2000	3000
		Yearly $ cost shown below.				
Cost per kilowatt hour	2¢	$7	$20	$28	$56	$84
	4¢	$14	$41	$56	$112	$168
	6¢	$20	$61	$80	$160	$240
	8¢	$27	$82	$108	$216	$324
	10¢	$34	$102	$136	$272	$408
	12¢	$41	$122	$163	$326	$489

Ask your salesperson or local utility for the energy rate (cost per kilowatt hour) in your area.

Important

Removal of this label before consumer purchase is a violation of federal law (42 U.S.C. 6302).

(Part No. 20648)

about energy. The results of this stage of the research were used to formulate the final labels that were quantitatively evaluated in a follow-up study.

Eight labels were prepared for each of three appliances, room air conditioner, refrigerator-freezers, and dishwashers. The variables studied were the label headings, the inclusion of a cost matrix or grid, and the method of presenting the comparative energy consumption data. Each of the variables had two treatments, resulting in a 2 x 2 x 2 factorial design (two headings x verbal or numeric presentation of costs x simple or complex method). The details of the methodology, together with the findings, are contained in <u>Communication Effectiveness of Energy Consumption Labels for Major Appliances</u> (Response Analysis Corporation 1977).

Each consumer in the study saw only one label for a single product. Twenty respondents were assigned to each of the 24 treatments, for a total sample of 480. Personal interviews were conducted in four cities, with consumers randomly assigned to treatments. An interview consisted of both attitudinal and cognitive measures, with an attempt made to determine the attractiveness and communicability of each of the formats.

Overall, respondents judged all of the alternatives highly. Few differences were found which differentiated the label formats. The more complex label format was finally selected because of its ability to communicate costs relevant to different consumers with no apparent detrimental effect on the comprehensibility of the central cost disclosure. It should be noted that the conclusiveness of the findings might be questioned by some, given the state of the art of consumer research in areas dealing with energy and conservation at the time of the study and considering the limited options presented to the Commission because of the limitations of the enabling legislation and the DOE tests.

Today, with the benefit of added insight into appliance purchasing behavior, the FTC is using consumer research to measure the effectiveness of the final regulation retrospectively. As a baseline measure -- it is anticipated that the labels will begin to appear on appliances in early 1980 -- telephone interviews were conducted with recent buyers of refrigerator-freezers and clothes washers who were members of a national consumer mail panel. Buyers were asked questions about their information seeking and evaluation of alternatives to determine the degree to which consumers seek out and use energy cost information in their buying decisions. The respondents were also asked about any labels they may have seen at the point of purchase which provided energy cost information. The study, which is currently in progress, will be replicated in 1981 to determine the degree to which consumers have recognized and used the information provided by the labels.

SUMMARY AND CONCLUSION

This paper has described a labeling program for conserving considerable amounts of increasingly scarce energy. Marketing techniques have been extensively utilized in designing the program. Its specific aims are to provide the information consumers need to make energy-conserving decisions, in a format which will maximize the use of the information by the maximum number of consumers.

The results of the program will be measured in the future. If it is successful, it will have encouraged an increased number of consumers to use energy cost in evaluating alternative appliances. This kind of consumer evaluation will give manufacturers incentives to make their appliances more energy efficient and to communicate such information to consumers in promotion and advertising. As a result, considerable benefits will be realized both through a saving of energy resources and through a creation of a new conservation ethic in the American consumer.

REFERENCES

Advertising Age (1978), "Pertschuk Lauds Appliance Industry For Role in Energy Cost Label Program," 49 (July 3), 4.

Consumer Reports (1979), "The Push for Energy-Efficient Appliances," (January), 28-29.

Energy Policy and Conservation Act (1975), Public Law 94-163, December 22.

Federal Trade Commission, Bureau of Consumer Protection (1979), Labeling and Advertising of Consumer Appliances, February.

FTC News Summary (1979), "FTC Approves Appliance Energy Rule," (July 6), 1.

National Energy Conservation Policy Act (1978), Public Law 95-619, November 9.

Response Analysis Corporation (1977), <u>Communication Effectiveness of Energy Consumption Labels for Major Appliances</u>, Study Conducted for the Federal Trade Commission, December.

PART THREE

CONSERVATION TODAY

This part deals with the present state of the art in the field of resource conservation and recovery; also takes up problems created by government regulations.

A SENSIBLE APPROACH TO RESOURCE CONSERVATION

Senator Lloyd Bentsen

INTRODUCTION

Before you switched to coffee or other spirits, I'm sure all of you drank milk from standard cartons. Most packaging companies still manufacture them the same old way. However, the International Paper Company has introduced a new type of carton, just as good, which reduces the amount of cardboard needed by 30 percent. It holds the same amount of milk yet it does so in a much more productive way than the industry has been accustomed to using.

Why has that company done this? Was it done for esthetic reasons, or was there a profit motive? The answer to that question is obvious. But that decision and hundreds of thousands of others just like it offer an answer to a much larger question: Can the world of profit sheets make a go of advancing environmental and resource conservation goals better than the world of regulatory sheets and rules? It is my hope that this conference will explore this question in depth; not so much in an either/or fashion -- either we leave environmental and resource preservation questions to the government or we let the freemarket hold reign -- but rather in terms of what can government and business do to most effectively meet our material needs in a way which is compatible with the environment. Resource utilization and resource conservation need not be mutually exclusive. There is a very large common ground.

U.S. RESOURCE UTILIZATION

We are a rich nation. And we make enormous demands on our environment and resources. In 1972, the United States consumed 290 million tons of forest products, 140 million tons of metals, 1.9 billion tons of fuel minerals, and 2.1 billion tons of nonmetallic, nonfuel materials. Since 1870, we have doubled our consumption of materials every 35 years. We now discard 160 million tons of materials per year, or approximately 4.5 pounds per person every day of the year.

For most of our history our economy stressed resource utilization over conservation and recovery. Resources were both cheap and abundant. And we knew that the faster we used our abundant materials, the faster we would build our economy and the economic well-being of our citizens. Present and future generations would benefit by turning minerals in the ground, trees in the forests and nonfood fibers in the fields into productive assets. So we used our God-given natural resources and, as a result, made our nation, by far, the wealthiest in the history of the world.

NATURAL RESOURCES AND RECYCLING

Recently, however, -- and business has seen this trend first -- there have been rising real costs associated with the extraction and processing of raw materials. The declining yield or increasing cost phenomenon for natural resources is most obvious in the case of petroleum because of OPEC pricing policies, which have magnified depletion-related cost increases. Little wonder, then, that recycling has gained favor with more and more firms. Elimination of extracting and most processing steps alone can cut energy use an average of 70 percent. The costs to business likewise are significantly reduced.

Market Inefficiencies

The marketplace serves as a mechanism to balance the use of virgin materials and recycled products. Yet, at the present time, there are market imperfections preventing real prices of new resources from being reflected in market prices, to the disadvantage of recycling. These inefficiencies are the result of the market system's inability to include environmental and disposal costs in product prices; and of distortions caused by the Federal regulatory system.

In the absence of these inefficiencies, the market would tend to favor recycling of materials and resources to a much greater extent than it presently does.

Federal Regulatory System. I'd like to concentrate on the second of these distoring influences, the effect of the Federal regulatory system on virgin and recycled material costs. As a member of the Senate Finance Committee, I am acutely aware of the many ways that the Federal Government can distort the economics of two competing products so that one, which may have been uneconomic, can compete favorably in the marketplace. These government actions include taxes as well as the plethora of bureaucratic mandates being emitted daily from Washington, particularly in the energy area. And, daily, business advocates of materials reuse confront market disadvantages because of these Federal regulatory intereferences with the marketplace.

An example in point involved the soaring demand several years ago for cellulose insulating materials and the use of recycled newsprint as a raw material. The Federal Trade Commission found flaws in the fire retardant characteristic of cellulose treated with sulfuric acid. That finding plunged the waste paper business into a severe recession. The FTC acted because it is obligated to protect consumers from hazardous or potentially hazardous products. Yet, neither the FTC nor anyone else encouraged a revamping of cellulose insulation technology to improve its fire retardant characteristic.

The result, as we all know, was the crippling of a new recycling industry, spot shortages, and soaring prices for badly needed insulating materials. With some imagination, a heavy-handed bureaucratic disruption of the marketplace could have been offset by a low-cost innovative solution to the need for inexpensive, effective and safe insulating materials.

New Trend in Regulation

We are seeing a positive trend -- now several years old -- toward some Federal regulations' favoring the use of recycled materials over virgin ones. For example, Section 6002 of the Resource Conservation and Recovery Act of 1976 mandates that all products purchased with Federal funds contain the highest percentage of recycled materials possible. The Environmental Protection Agency is currently working on guidelines for implementing this law. It could well result in Federal agencies' occasionally purchasing recycled items that are more expensive than virgin ones, even though such calculations are extremely difficult to make in practice, inasmuch as market prices for virgin goods may not accurately reflect replacement costs. In any case, Congress certainly has acknowledged, through this and other recycle provisions, that it is time for our economy to aggressively overcome its bias against recycled versus virgin resources. That is a very positive statement of fact.

Cyclical Problem

However, further government action to prod the market is called for and even necessary, because of the cyclical nature of most raw material industries.

With relatively high fixed costs and low variable costs, extractive industries tend to maintain a given production rate within an extremely wide price range. Yet, the production of recycled substitutes is price-sensitive and is profitable, generally, only at the upper end of raw material price ranges. Consequently, a marked degree of instability exists in their demand, with abnormally severe cycles typically found for most recycled goods.

This exaggerated cyclical behavior is greatly magnified by government regulations. In the previous example of newspaper recycling, the demand for used newspapers soared as weather-insulation manufacturers sought cellulose as a raw material. During this boom, the price of newsprint went from the normal $10 per ton to anywhere from $40 to $60 per ton. These high prices had the desired effect, as independent scavengers and others, notably civic groups, responded with floods of surplus paper.

The FTC's action questioning the flammability of cellulose insulation, however, sent the newspaper recycling business reeling. Currently, newspaper is selling in Washington, D. C. for as little as $6 per ton. People who had become accustomed to doing something useful with their Sunday papers on Monday couldn't find a convenient drop-off point as collection centers closed, or couldn't make enough money to cover their fixed costs, especially gasoline.

So it is incumbent on government to minimize the adverse impact on recycled products of its rules and regulations. And when a conflict is unavoidable, then I believe the government must be flexible enough, and imaginative enough, to help resolve the conflict without causing inflation and aggravating shortages.

Incidentally, in the case of paper recycling, let me add that not all is gloom. Garden State Paper Company has recently made it a policy to use only recycled fibers in manufacturing newsprint. It has opened a new papermill in Athens, Georgia, to supply newspaper companies with a dependable source of paper. And it is projected that, as the mill grows -- and with the unprecedented demand for newsprint in the South, it doubtlessly will grow -- the high prices Garden State will be offering for old newspapers will allow recycling programs to spring up and prosper throughout that part of the country without government help or interference.

Unfortunately, Garden State is an exception. It is not difficult to understand why businesses, like Garden State and the International Paper Company, are the exception rather than the rule -- why most businesses still use virgin over recycled materials. The cost of raw materials in many cases is artificially kept low. We have seen that oil, as a raw material, has been priced well below replacement costs. Such a price level has encouraged and continues to encourage a higher-than-normal usage of petroleum than would otherwise be dictated by the market. It has seriously debilitated energy conservation programs and left us dangerously vulnerable to foreign manipulation of our domestic economy and foreign policy. It has also seriously delayed efforts to develop acceptable substitutes.

PRODUCTIVITY AND RECYCLING

In addition to market instability and price distortions, there are other biases against recycled products. For example, productivity in recycling operations is generally less than it is in extractive and materials processing work. The capital-to-labor ratio is lower. So an hour of labor spent in manufacturing raw materials tends to be cheaper per unit of output than one spent in recycling materials.

Put another way, assembly line efficiencies and economies of scale help keep labor costs down in traditional extractive and processing industries; whereas, recycling is relatively labor-intensive, is done on a small scale and, therefore, is most costly per unit of output. In effect, the recycling genre faces productivity problems--as, indeed, does our entire economy.

Poor Productivity Record

Since World War II, our economy has scored one of the worst productivity records of the industrialized nations. In 1950, it took seven Japanese or three Germans to match the output of one American worker. But as these and other nations saved and invested heavily, as they devoted growing portions of their national wealth to research and development and as we here deflected badly needed capital away from productive uses with government rules and regulations, the productivity gap shrank. Today, it takes only two Japanese or 1.3 Germans to match one American's production. And if present trends continue--with productivity growth here well below that even of Great Britain--productivity in Canada, Japan, Germany, and Italy will soon surpass ours. And that just means more inflation, a stagnating pool of domestic goods and services, a declining dollar on foreign exchange markets, and continuing job loss abroad. It is a prescription for economic disaster.

Reversing Trend

We have to reverse this trend in falling productivity. And we have to do it in a fashion which promotes productivity in the manufacture of recycled as well as virgin products. That means an emphasis on R&D and particularly R&D by smaller, newer companies. It is with these objectives in mind that I drafted and recently submitted two bills designed to stimulate R&D by smaller companies. Both bills, "The Research Promotion Act" (S. 1256) and "The Research Tax Incentive Act" (S. 1257), provide additional after-tax dollars to smaller firms who plow back a sizable portion of their sales receipts into research.

Improved productivity will hold the cost of recycled products down. And it is the key answer to the cost disadvantage which recycled products are now perceived to have. But it is a long-term answer.

In the short run, the government--and here I mean the Federal, as well as State and local government--must learn to keep its regulatory hands out of the marketplace unless it is willing to promote positive solutions to perceived problems. It can play a positive, solid role--with revised tax and materials pricing policies, for example--and with other incentives designed to stimulate the increased use of recycled products. But it also must review the plethora of rules and regulations that discourage recycling at the expense of the utilization of virgin materials. Our national resource base is well served by the promotion of recycling. And that objective is best served through the use of government incentives rather than regulatory dictates. Incentives, not coercion, is the proper approach.

HISTORICAL SKETCH OF RESOURCE RECOVERY AND STATUS OF ENERGY RETRIEVAL FROM WASTE

Ronald E. Schwegler, Browning-Ferris Industries

INTRODUCTION

Each year, whenever the solid waste management industry gathers to hold a convention, seminar or symposium, invariably some portion of the program contains a paper or panel discussion on the subject of resource recovery. In the past, many proponents of resource recovery have adhered to a concept which is not unlike that of the alchemist, but instead of gold from lead, they now seek gold out of garbage.

In the early days of resource recovery, at the inception of the gold-from-garbage principle, if a person spoke out questioning any facet of the program such as reliability, environmental acceptance or cost effectiveness, he was immediately looked upon as an antagonist intent on doing bodily harm to this infant industry. Now that nearly a decade has passed since the inception of pioneering work in resource recovery, it is much easier to understand the outspoken concerns of the early constructive critics of the technology.

HISTORICAL SKETCH

As background to an understanding of resource recovery today, this paper presents a historical sketch and an update organized around various time periods classified into four "isms" or states.

1968 to 1972--Optimism

During this period, literally anyone with a concept or pilot plant who had conceived or semi-demonstrated the ability to retrieve a particle of energy from wood chips, corn husks, rice hulls or macadamia nuts announced to the nation that they had the total solution to our solid waste management problems.

The Federal Government, through its new Environmental Protection Agency office, opened the doors to the bank so that the necessary capital needed by the entrepreneurs would provide for the immediate replacement of the land-filling system for solid waste disposal.

1973 to 1975--Skepticism

This was an era of confusion due to the fact that the promised new technologies had not come to fruition; the landfill was still all too visible. Why, with all the infusion of the federal and state grant monies, hadn't the new technologies brought us to a better system?

There had been those within the solid waste industry who had predicted that we were running too fast into the forest and would all too soon be lost. If they should be right, when would we eventually regain the required sense of direction? Skepticism ranged over the industry.

1975 to 1977--Pessimism

This time period witnessed the abandonment of the almost 20 million dollar Monsanto pyrolysis project in Baltimore, Maryland. The withdrawal by Monsanto left many communities, then considering resource recovery alternatives to solid waste disposal, to question their future role.

One must realize that when a community is servicing revenue bonds for a facility that is not functioning at designed capacity, while at the same time is left with the additional cost problem of refuse disposal, that it does not make for a very tranquil atmosphere.

During this same time period in St. Louis, the 8,000 ton per day proposed Union Electric Company's refuse-to-energy project was curtailed. This multi-million dollar project had received so much national attention that its abandonment further heightened the industry's pessimistic concerns as to whether or not any of the new technologies could ever be counted upon as an effective alternative for disposal.

UPDATE AND EVALUATION

1979 to ?--Realism

Today, we are just now emerging from a forest of confusion with a clearer view of what is ahead. We now understand that there is not any single panacea to our disposal problems. It is recognized that success in finding solutions to such problems takes a tremendous dedication on the part of the proponents of the new technologies. It requires vast sums of capital commitments in order to initiate disposal systems. It requires a community supportive of the efforts being expended by the solid waste industry. Equally recognized is the fact that the required partner for any resource recovery project is and forever will be the sanitary landfill. One will not exist without the other.

Most important of all, there is widespread appreciation of the key factors that will make resource recovery alternatives more competitive. They include the strong combination of increased costs of land disposal--required by new federal and state criteria for waste disposal--and escalating energy costs. Another key factor is the enforced separation of land-filling sites from collection areas.

True, a number of large firms have made the necessary sizeable commitments of capital and have shown exemplary dedication to resource recovery. This number includes American Can, Black-Clawson, Boeing, Occidental Petroleum, Raytheon and Teledyne National. Notwithstanding the extensive efforts of these firms, the resource recovery industry is still not economically competitive, owing to difficult problems encountered in handling refuse. Hence, it is near impossible to expect under-capitalized firms to step forward and solve problems that have plagued the large firms. Yet, in most major metropolitan areas, there are still persons who feel, for whatever reason, that they can solve the problems unsolved by the giants of the industry. Even today the federal government keeps making grants to Rube Goldbergs promising to save the industry.

STATUS OF ENERGY RETRIEVAL FROM WASTE

Each year, I review all active resource recovery efforts and personally visit newly emerging facilities in order to track their progress. For the past four years, each review has been presented at the annual American Public Works Association (APWA) Congress. The audience at the Congress basically consists of city managers and directors of public works who are feeling the public pressure to create resource recovery facilities at the earliest moment. Various parts of the review presented in November of 1978 at the APWA Congress in Boston are summarized in three tables. (The 1979 review was presented in Portland, Oregon and will be published soon by the Institute for Solid Waste of the APWA.)

The approach to recovering energy from refuse falls basically into three categories, around which the review tables are organized. Table 1 reviews the status of recovery systems based on <u>pyrolysis</u>, which is the distillation of organic material in the absence of oxygen; Table 2, systems based on <u>water-walled combustion</u>, which is the buring of refuse whose

TABLE 1

1978 STATUS OF ENERGY RECOVERY BY PYROLYSIS SYSTEMS

Project Location & Start-Up Date	Developer	Process Name	Design Capacity	Energy Product & Reported BTU Value	Other Resources Recovered
S. Charleston, West Virginia 1974	Union Carbide Corp. Linde Div. 1	PUROX System	200 T/D	Gas 20,000 cu.ft./ton. Refuse @300 BTU/ cu.ft.	Front end ferrous metal recovery. Sterile granular aggregate residue.
El Cajon, California 1977	Occidental Research Corp. (ORC)	Garrett Process	200 T/D	Oil one barrel/ton. Refuse @4.8 x 10 BTU/barrel.	Front end recovery of ferrous metals, glass, aluminum.
Santa Ana, California	Enterprise Company	Deco Process	50 T/D	Gas/oil. Barrel oil per ton refuse	Front end recovery of ferrous metals, possible Al from char residue.
Baltimore, Maryland	Monsanto Envirochem	formerly Landgard	1000 T/D	Steam 2000,000 lb/hr @100-200 psig 415°F (Steam customer Baltimore Gas & Electric Co.)	
(See Review)	Torrax Systems, Inc. & Andco, Inc.	Andco		(See Review) Steam	

Source: Institute for Solid Wastes, American Public Works Association

TABLE 2

1978 STATUS OF ENERGY RECOVERY BY WATER-WALLED COMBUSTION SYSTEMS

Project Location & Start-Up Date	Developer	Process Name Stoker/Grate Mfg.	Design Capacity	Energy Products
Nashville, Tennessee 1974	Nashville Thermal Transfer Corp.	Thermal Detroit Stoker Co.	720 T/D	Steam 270,000 lb/hr @400 psig/600°F. (Steam used for heating and cooling downtown bldgs.)
Saugus, Massachusetts 1976	Wheelabrator Frye, Inc.	RESCO Von Roll	150 T/D	Steam 370,000 lb/hr @ 890 psig/875°F. (Steam customer--General Electric Power Plant)
Quebec City, Quebec, Canada summer, 1974	Quebec City	NA Von Roll	1000 T/D	Steam 162,000 lb/hr@ 680 psig/600°F. (Steam customer-Anglo Pulp Co.)
Chicago, Illinois	City of Chicago	Northwest Incinerator Josef Martin	1600 T/D	Steam 440,000 lb/hr @ 275 psig/414°F (No market for steam)
Harrisburg, Pennsylvania 9/27/75	Harrisburg Incinerator Authority	Harrisburg Incinerator Josef Martin	720 T/D	Steam 150,000 lb/hr @ 250 psig/460°F (No market for steam)

Source: Institute for Solid Wastes, American Public Works Association

TABLE 1

1978 STATUS OF ENERGY RECOVERY BY PYROLYSIS SYSTEMS

Project Capital Cost	Review Update November 1978
$15,000,000 (estimated research expenditures to date)	During 1977-78 co-disposal (refuse/sewage sludge) tests were conducted under program partially funded by EPA. Air emission tests, utilizing Los Angeles area standards, were conducted under program partially funded by State of California. Due to excessive testing costs for operation of the full scale modular plant in S. Charleston, virtually all future tests will be conducted at the newly constructed 10 ton per day facility in Tonawanda, NY. Marketing the process continued to present difficulties during past year.
$15,000,000	Since July 1978 ORC virtually suspended all testing programs on the flash pyrolysis process due to identified operational problems which would necessitate additional substantial capital expenditures to correct. Plant was not able to achieve a continuous 70 hour test run as was required by EPA contract. Bechtel Corp. reportedly has been retained by ORC to review the entire process. Testing of the 50 ton per day modular unit was completed during spring of 1978. Numerous modifications were made in an attempt to increase the thru-put capacity and overall performance. Air pollution problems were evident during most of the testing. An approximate total of 300 tons of materials was processed during testing. Unit is currently being dismantled for removal from test site. Future project unknown at this time.
$30,000,000	City of Baltimore assumed total responsibility of the 1000 ton per day (design capactiy) when Monsanto withdrew from the project early in 1977. Plant was operated, by City forces, from latter part of 1977 until March, 1978 at an approximate daily volume of 600 tons per day. The March, 1978 shutdown was necessitated to permit numerous modifications to the facility. An electrostatic precipitator has now been installed together with a larger gas purifier and a 220 foot high discharge stack in an attempt to eliminate air pollution problems inherent with the original plant. The storage site has been re-worked to permit access by a skiploader for assured retrieval of the shredded fuel product. Plant should shortly be on line again.
N/A	a) Luxembourg - Facility has been operated at approximately 200 t/d over past 12 months. Plant received major modifications after initial construction. This plant was first commercial installation. b) Grasse, France - Facility has been operated at approximately 170 tons per day over past 12 months. Steam produced being sold to major perfume manufacturer. c) Frankfort, Germany - 200 tons per day facility currently undergoing start-up OS/EPA reportedly interested in working with West German government to develop a test program utilizing U.S. standards. d) Cretel, France - a 400 tons per day plant currently under construction is scheduled for mid 1979 completion.

TABLE 2

1978 STATUS OF ENERGY RECOVERY BY WATER WALLED COMBUSTION SYSTEMS

Projected Capital Cost	Review-Update October
$25,000,000	Facility has operated during past year at an approximate 400-ton-per-day level. Newly installed electrostatic precipitators permit units to meet all applicable air emission standards of the area. Steam being sold for heating and cooling of downtown buildings.
$50,000,000	Approximately 4.5 billion pounds of steam have been sold to General Electric since plant start-up in 1976. Total waste processed during this period was approximately 850,000 tons. Current tipping fee for refuse is $14.20 per ton. Air emission problems occurring in summer 1978 were traced to black carbon flakes being emitted from the plant due to the inability of the flakes to hold an electrical charge. A test program and experimentation has now virtually eliminated the problem and has allowed for removal of an operating restriction placed upon the facility during the problem period.
$25,000,000	Successful steam sales program has permitted tipping fees to be held at an approximate $10.00-per-ton rate.
$30,000,000	Operating at approximate 1000-ton-per-day level. Contract has been let for construction of a 14-inch line for delivery of the product to a major candy manufacturer. Reported price to be paid for steam is around $2.40 per 1000 lbs.
$8,300,000	Operating at approximate 500-tons-per-day level. Although no steam sales have been achieved to date, a new 14-inch diameter, 2.4-mile steam line currently under construction will permit future sale of the product. Cost of the steam line was contracted at approximately $4,000,000.

TABLE 3

1978 STATUS OF ENERGY RECOVERY BY REFUSE-DERIVED FUEL SYSTEMS

Project Location & Start-Up Date	Developer	Market for Fuel	Design Capcity	Energy Product	Other Resources Recovered	Estimated Costs
Ames, Iowa November, 1975	Gibbs, Hill Durham & Richardson, Inc.	Ames Municipal Power Plant	200T/D	Shredded, air classified solid waste fuel	Ferrous metal, aluminum, glass	$6,500,000
Milwaukee, Wisconsin 8/15/75	Americology	Wisconsin Electric Power, Co. (WEPCO)	100T/D	Shredded, air classified solid waste fuel	Ferrous metal, aluminum, glass	$18,000,000
Baltimore County, Maryland 8/26/75	Teledyne National	None	400-1200T/D	Two classes of shredded, air classified solid waste	Ferrous metal, non-ferrous metal, glass	$10,000
New Orleans, Louisiana March 1978	Waste Management Inc.	Under investigation	650T/D	Shredded, air-classified solid waste fuel	Ferrous metal, glass, aluminum, paper	$6,300,000
Chicago, Illinois 10/3/75	Ralph M. Parsons Co. Consoer, Townsend & Associates	Commonwealth Edison, Crawford Power Station	100T/D	Shredded, air classified solid waste fuel	Ferrous metal, provisions for future non-ferrous recovery	$20,000,000 (estimated)
Lane County, Oregon 8/18/77	Allis-Chaimers	Unknown	500T/D	Shredded, air classified solid waste fuel	Ferrous metals	$2,200,000
Toronto, Ontario, Canada 2/10/77	Ontario Ministry. the Environment	Fuel to be. burned in small boiler to heat plant	800T/D	Shredded, air classified solid waste fuel	Ferrous metal, glass,	$13,600,000
Hempstead, New York 9/26/75	Black-Clawson	N/A	2000T/D	Steam (Probable steam customer-Long Island Lighting Co.	Ferrous metal, aluminum, glass	$55,000,000
Tacoma, Washington October 1978	Tacoma	N/A	500T/D	Shredded, air classified solid waste fuel	Ferrous	$2.4 million (see review)
Monroe, County, New York 8/19/75	Raytheon Service Company	Rochester Gas & Electric Co.	2000T/D	Shredded, air classified solid waste fuel	Ferrous metals aluminum, glass	$28,500,000
Bridgeport, Connecticut 8/28/75	Combustion Equipment Assoc., Inc., & Occidental Research Corp. (ORC)	Northeast Utilities Devon Power Plant (contracts unsigned)	1500T/D	Shredded, air classified ball-milled solid waste fuel (Eco-Fuel II)	Ferrous metal, aluminum, glass	$22,000,000
Akron, Ohio 10/6/75	Glaus, Pyle, Schomen, Burns and DeHaven	Unknown	1000T/D	Shredded, air classified solid waste fuel fuel	Ferrous metal, provisions for future non-ferrous recovery	$21,000,000
Niagara Falls, New York	Glaus, Pyle, Schomen, Burns and De Haven	Hooker Chemical Corp.	2500-3000T/D	Shredded, air classified solid waste fuel/steam	Ferrous	$80,000,000 (estimated)

Source: Institute for Solid Wastes, American Public Works Association

TABLE 3

1978 STATUS OF ENERGY RECOVERY BY REFUSE-DERVIED FUEL SYSTEMS

Review-Update

Past year contracts were let for retrofitting existing facility with dust collection system, rotary disc screens, and dump grates in the suspension-fired boiler. All material now going to suspension-fired boiler retrofittied with dump grates. Reportedly installation of disc screens has eliminated previous slagging problems. The RDF storage bin floor, having been replaced once, is again in need of replacement. Disposal cost for refuse is reported at between $12 and $13 per ton after all credits.

Plant continued intermittently to process approximately 800 tons per day past 12 months. Current tipping fee at $11.20 per ton. Aluminum retrieval began in August 1978. Ferrous recovery reportedly consistent at about 6%. RDF sales to WEPCO averaging 400 to 500 tons per day at a value set at approximately $1.10 per million BTUs. Plant was modified by the addition of rotary disc screen in an attempt to eliminate boiler slagging problems and conveyor belts widened to increase overall plant efficiency. In the past a restrictive policy concerning depth reviews/visits to the facility had existed. This policy is currently being re-examined by Americology. Since this facility represents a key link in the progress of recovery, it should be included in any overall review.

Plant processed approximately 700 tons per day during past year. Tipping fee set at $8 per ton for commercial haulers, residential material received at no charge (handled through property tax). There have been no aluminum sales to date. Ferrous retrieval continues to average approximately 4%. Currently selling approximately 10 tons per day of RDF to major paper company for boiler testing. EPA reportedly has contracted for purchase of 1000 tons of pellitized refuse to conduct further tests. June 1978 new transfer station approximately 15 miles distant from process plant went on line to supply 250-300 tons per day of material to process facility.

Plant continues to receive and process approximately 650 tons per day at a tipping fee of $11.66 per ton. Construction of the overall resource recovery facilities were certified complete on March 1, 1978. Aluminum currently being processed with no sales to date. The glass recovery portion of the facility is in final stages of start-up. Ferrous retrieval approximates 3.5% of incoming volumn. No RDF sales have been afforded as yet.

An estimated $20 million now has been expended at the facility which has undergone 15 months of start-up operations. Plant continues to be operated intermittently at a 400-ton-per-day level. Problems occurring in the air lock system and with the acceptability of particle size of the shredded product have been major holdups. Edison now reportedly has accepted the product quality.

Plant started contractual shakedown operations inspring of 1978. Two major problems identified at that time were vibrating screens from primary shredders' inability to provide level feed to the air classifier and plugging in screen conveyors from air classifier to surge hoppers. The thru-put capacity of system is affected by these problems. EPA has awarded the project a $220,000 grant for technical, economical, and environmental evaluation of the facility. Terms call for paying a fee to the operator of $4.14 per incoming ton, which further calls for 85% of all resource recovery revenues to be retained by by the County. No sales contracts for the RDF have yet been signed.

The Ontario Ministry, through a $13.8-million environmental grant, constructed a full-scale experimental resource recovery plant which will provide for an evaluation of all technical and economical aspects of operating such facilities. The facility features a transfer station which has been handling approximately 1000 tons per day over the past year. Plant will produce baled cardboard and paper, ferrous and non-ferrous metals, glass, organic fibers, compost materials, and an RDF fraction. A 50-ton-per-day co-disposal compost digestion system, extensive dust control, and operation of a small Consumat boiler system are but a few of the experimental highlights of the plant. The facility, which is privately operated, permits one of the most open door review policies existing within the industry. A must on your list of facilities to visit.

In August, 1978, one half of the plant's 2000 ton-per-day-design capacity started a shakedown program. The plant features a wet pulverizing process utilizing technology adapted from paper industry. The final RDF represented one of the most homogeneous materials viewed to date. One boiler was being test fired during the October 1978 visit. Several minor material-handling problems have been identified and are being corrected by Black Clawson, owner/operator of the facility. It is estimated that the tipping fee will be in the $16-per-ton range. The City of Hempstead will receive a 40% rebate from residual products. A 6-month time period has been projected for the shakedown period. This facility also represents a major role in the resource recovery industry and a must to see in the future.

The $2.4 million construction cost for the plant did not include financing for the 800-horsepower shredder and receiving area, which previously had been owned and operated by the city. The unique feature of the facility is a newly designed air separation system which utilizes engineering principals of a tailored air stream. The air classifier was designed and patented and is owned by the Boeing Co. of Seattle. No contracts for the sale of RDF have yet been effected. The facility is currently undergoing start-up operations.

The 2000-ton-per-day facility, located in Rochester, New York, and designed by the Raytheon Service Co., was approximately 95% complete in October 1978, when reviewed. Special features of the truly awesome facility include very sophisticated shredding and air classification. A proprietary aluminum separation system, developed by Raytheon, and froth flotation glass recovery systems are also featured. The approximate $50 million construction costs were financed by General Obligations Bonds backed by the New York State Department of Environmental Conservation.

Construction started-in December 1976, under terms of a very restrictive time schedule (23 months allowed for completion), which is now recognized by most to have been unrealistic. Original tipping fee set @$12.95 per ton as tied to August 1974 C.P.I. would now be estimated at approximately $16 per ton. Approximately 1200 tons per day of refuse has now been contracted; additional cities are being recruited. The glass recovery portion of the facility is currently being held in abeyance to facilitate further review into the marketability of the product on a cost-effective basis. The RDF fuel product achieved by the CEAOXY process is considered by this writer as one of the finest of all such products in the industry and should be very adaptable to existing boiler installations with little or no required modifications. This facility should be on the must see list for anyone truly interested in resource recovery. The next year should provide the necessary data to evaluate the overall system complete with cost information.

The plant is presently approximately 85% completed. Hydrostatic testing of one of the three semi-suspension fired boilers has been completed. The plant is scheduled for start-up by summer 1979. The important issue in Akron, now in the hands of the court, revolved around the ownership of collected refuse.

Hooker Chemical Corp., a wholly owned subsidiary of Occidental Petroleum Corp., has funded the design and construction for the 2500-3000 ton-per-day RDF plant. The project, which could have a total price tag approximating $80-$90 million (including finance charges) will feature two 300,000 lb./hour boilers for a 13.8 kv electrical supply to be utilized at their own facilities. Hooker engineers are projecting an approximate $10-per-ton tipping fee upon completion of the plant, scheduled for spring 1980.

heat is used to generate steam from boiler tubes hung within the fire chamber; Table 3, systems based on <u>refuse-derived fuel</u>, which is the upgrading and refining of refuse which can act as an auxiliary fuel for a conventionally fired boiler or as the main fuel for new boilers designed to use this lower BTU product.

Pyrolysis is by far the most sophisticated of the three technologies. To date is has not been used in any commercially successful installation in the United States. Water-walled combustion, which has enjoyed considerable success in the European marketplace, has not been used much in the United States, probably due to our more restrictive air pollution laws. Refuse-derived fuel (RDF) has and is receiving the lion's share of attention in the refuse-to-energy field. One problem with the RDF concept of energy retrieval is that the cost effectiveness of this technology is unknown. The industry is anxiously waiting for more cost information to be developed in order to properly assess the future role of RDF in solid waste management.

ALUMINUM AND OUR ENVIRONMENT

David P. Reynolds, Reynolds Metals Company

Aluminum is the most plentiful metal in the earth's crust, and it also may be the most plentiful metal in space. Lunar ore, for instance, is rich in aluminum.

Here on earth, aluminum ranks second only to steel in terms of its widespread use. Its versatility makes it an important and essential part of our homes, our cars, our packaging, our transportation systems, our electrical distribution network, our industry and our leisure and recreational pursuits.

Recently, a prominent magazine carried an article entitled "Aluminum, the Magic Metal." It said that "just as earlier ages of human development have taken their names from the distinctive material that nurtured them -- Stone, Bronze, Iron -- there are those who believe our era may be called the "Aluminum Age." (National Geographic 1978, p. 188.)

Yet, in spite of all of the contributions aluminum is making to our world today, I would be willing to bet that if you were to ask most Americans the first word that comes to their mind today when they think of aluminum, the response would be "recycling."

ECOLOGICAL MARKETING PROGRAMS AT REYNOLDS

Ten years ago at Reynolds we started consumer recycling on a pilot scale because we felt that the aluminum can, by virtue of its high scrap value, could be its own incentive for its return and re-use. Our primary objective was helping those who yearned for a cleaner America by trying to alleviate the litter and solid waste problem. By making it convenient for the public to return the cans, and paying them for the metal, we also thought it would be a way to help those who needed to supplement their incomes or to help organizations raise funds for worthy causes. We also looked on it as an intelligent way to conserve a valuable resource, and to supplement our metal supply.

Recycling, because it is both good business and good citizenship, because it helps others, has succeeded beyond our wildest dreams.

It has grown into a nationwide business for us and has resulted in similar programs by other companies and industries.

It has given us the opportunity to lead the way in the promotion and advancement of the cause of recycling, as a solution, not only to the problems of litter and waste, but to the conservation of energy and resources.

For decades, recycling has been a persistent and developing theme in the history of our company. In the 1940's we developed a way to reclaim and recycle foil from packaging laminates. Right after the war, we were literally forging swords into plowshares by recycling World War II aircraft into farm buildings. In the 1950's we experimented with recycling used oil cans. These were innovative programs for their day. But the amount of metal we are recycling today is staggering by comparison. The capacity of our new Recycling and Reclamation Division surpasses the total annual amount of aluminum produced in this country in 1939 on the eve of World War II.

Recycling conserves resources and provides an important domestic supplement to our metal supply. And because each time aluminum is recycled, you save 95 percent of the energy required to make aluminum from ore, it conserves energy over and over again. In 1978, for example, Reynolds recycling efforts conserved about one billion kilowatt hours of electricity.

Since the inception of the program, we at Reynolds have recycled more than 14 billion cans and have paid the public more than $100 million for joining with us in the effort to conserve resources and energy.

Our Recycling and Reclamation Division involves 800 people, 80 permanent centers and physical facilities with assets in the neighborhood of $50 million. It operates at more than 875 collection points and does business in all fifty states, the District of Columbia and Puerto Rico.

Our Alabama Smelter recently processed its one billionth pound of recycled metal in less than 10 years of operation -- and a new expansion of that facility is now underway.

In 1978 alone we recycled 3.2 billion aluminum beverage cans and paid the public over $25 million to recycle cans and other clean household aluminum.

But the most gratifying thing to me is that recycling recognizes a human need, the concern of millions of individuals for a cleaner America and an end to the waste of our resources.

Municipal Resource Recovery

As we worked to develop the consumer recycling program, we also became interested in the vast potential that exists in municipal resource recovery. Three billion pounds of aluminum are being thrown away each year -- an amount equal to the entire U.S. output in 1958.

As a result, we have developed technology and systems to extract aluminum from the solid waste, or municipal refuse, stream -- as well as from junked automobiles. We helped to establish the National Center for Resource Recovery. We work closely with communities around the nation to ensure that aluminum recovery is included in resource recovery programs -- and to obtain long-term contracts to purchase aluminum recovered from municipal waste processing operations.

Earlier this year we began receiving shipments of recovered aluminum from New Orleans and Hempstead, Long Island.

Recycled House

To demonstrate in an imaginative way that a ready market exists for all kinds of reclaimed materials -- not just aluminum -- we built a recycled house in Richmond six years ago. It contained not only products made from recycled aluminum, but products made from fly ash, old newspapers, old rubber tires, and from fabric, wood and marble scrap. Even the yard was composted with recycled New York City garbage.

The house is conventional in appearance and was sold on the conventional real estate market after it was completed.

And it is a good example of how individual companies, within their own areas of expertise, can help solve some of the problems that face us today. By developing our ecological marketing concept through recycling and by others mustering their individual resources, by concentrating on particular areas, a positive contribution can be made that makes good business as well as good social sense in the conserver society.

In this context I would like to tell you about some other things we are doing.-- since Professor Henion in his original invitation gave me the latitude also to talk about other subjects being addressed by this conference.

Energy Conservation and Other Contributions

We have had our research people busy, for instance, looking at all the ways our material -- aluminum -- can help to solve the energy problem. The list is almost endless, and the energy savings are dramatic. In 1979 autos, aluminum will help save up to three billion gallons of gasoline over the life of these models alone. Aluminum in solar energy systems could reduce water and space heating fuel consumption in the average American home by as much as 60 percent. We are just beginning to see the potential contribution aluminum can make in these areas, and many others.

We have also looked at ways in which we can reduce the amount of energy it takes to make aluminum. Several years ago, based on 1972 consumption, the whole industry voluntarily committed to the federal government that it would reduce the amount of energy needed to make a pound of aluminum by 10 percent by 1980. That goal today has been exceeded -- a year ahead of schedule. And we are continuing to press forward.

In searching for a more effective way for the private sector to impact on the problem of the nation's unemployed, handicapped and disadvantaged minorities, our company has begun training some of these individuals as installers of our solar hot water systems. This program has great potential. We are very optimistic about our solar products, and we provide quality training. The net result will be expanded markets, improved earnings potential and a better qualified work force. If this example can be duplicated throughout the country, it will give great meaning to this total program.

We are proud of the contributions we have been able to make in the field of "Ecological Marketing." The situations I have mentioned are clearly cases in which "everybody wins," and they are the kind of things that can be multiplied many times over by the number of corporations and business firms in America.

I must point out, however, that these things did not happen by themselves. No program, no matter how ecologically sound, no matter if it has the "everybody wins" factor, can succeed unless the conserver society gets the message -- and that's where ecological marketing comes in.

SUMMARY AND CONCLUSIONS

In our recycling program, our reclamation efforts, the building of the recycled house, the employment of solar installers -- in each of these programs we have been able to maintain a steady and increasing flow of positive public attention for our programs.

Our marketing involves the basic tenet of public relations and advertising -- that _deeds_ as well as _words_ must be present to reinforce the credibility of the program. Or to put it another way, we must have both the action and communications to make the program effective.

We are now in the third phase of marketing our consumer

recycling program. When we started in 1967 we were in the pioneering period. Our primary objective was to demonstrate publicly that the aluminum can, far from being a litter menace, could help alleviate the problem of beverage container litter. We also had the assignment, as all ecological marketers must, to "educate" the public both in the philosophical area of the recycling ethic, and in the more prosaic area of how to recognize the difference between a steel and aluminum can.

In the early seventies, we moved to phase two -- the "major expansion period." By that time society had caught on to the recycling ethic. The company had been able to prove that recycling worked, and took it nationwide within a year and a half by opening up 70 new centers and expanding to more than 800 collection points.

Today our marketing efforts are in the "competitive era," our network is in place and other companies are coming into the business almost as rapidly as we expanded nationally in the past.

It is my fervent hope that these kinds of programs can continue to be discovered, nurtured and grow -- growing without the threat of government mandate or regulation. The private sector of our society offers the best seedbed for the blossoming of man's greatest accomplishments for the continued improvement of the world of today. In short, it offers the best chance for the harvest of the future.

REFERENCE

National Geographic (1978), "Aluminum, the Magic Metal," (August), 186-211.

RECYCLING: YESTERDAY'S IMAGE BUILDER IS TODAY'S INSURANCE POLICY

F. Lewis Shirley, Coors Container Company

A TRADITION OF EXCELLENCE

The words "recycling" and "conservation" have been around a long time at Adolph Coors Company, the nation's fifth largest brewer despite its limited marketing area of 16 western states. The reason is Adolph Coors was not a man to waste anything that could be used again. Not even an old, used cement sack.

In 1915, Coors saved 200 cement sacks and recycled each one of them. Adolph Coors even assigned his son to look for the one missing sack of 200 until it was found. He never did anything halfway. Over the years, that concern for conservation and the environment had been carried on at Coors. The company is the nation's fifth largest brewer despite its limited marketing area of 16 western states. It is now headed by the founder's grandsons, William K. Coors, chairman of the board and chief executive officer, and Joseph Coors, president and chairman of Coors Porcelain Company and Coors Container Company, the parent firm's two major wholly-owned subsidiaries.

So it is not surprising that in 1978--more than 100 years since Adolph Coors, with a partner he later bought out, opened the doors of the small brewery in the Rocky Mountain foothills just west of Denver--Coors had recovered 85 percent of all the aluminum cans it used. Some nine billion aluminum cans were recycled that year, totalling a staggering 90 million pounds. In fact, almost one-third of America's recycled aluminum cans were recovered by Coors.

Efforts like these have earned the company achievement awards from the Environmental Protection Agency and the Federal Energy Administration. And, throughout those decades, the company has been as proud of its environmental quality programs as it has been of its beer, traditionally the brand leader in its marketing area.

Today, Adolph Coors Company markets its products, including Coors and Coors Light beer, in aluminum cans, kegs and glass bottles. The packaging mix consits of 70 percent aluminum. No question about it, aluminum is Coors' choice to carry the load of its packaging requirements. But that didn't come about overnight. After years of research, aluminum was chosen by Coors as an ideal packaging material.

TWO MILESTONES

Sketched below is the historical background of two important developments that unfolded over the course of almost 20 years.

The Birth of the Aluminum Can

In the early 1950s Coors management recognized the unique properties of aluminum: compatibility with beer, light weight for shipping economy, superior heat transfer for efficient and rapid cooling and recyclability. Coors chose this metal for what was to become a remarkable, pioneering effort to produce aluminum beverage containers.

Joining forces with Chicago-based Beatrice Foods Company, Coors formed Aluminum International, Inc. to make 12-ounce extruded aluminum cans. Shortly thereafter, through continuing development, a primitive production line at Coors Porcelain Company was transforming silver dollar-sized aluminum slugs into 7-ounce cans designed by Coors. That small production line produced its own continuous cast and rolled aluminum stock. It was the beginning, the birth of the Coors aluminum can. Coors engineers recognized that it was only a start, and they continued development at an accelerated pace to make refinements and, eventually, another breakthrough--the draw and iron two-piece can. After six years and thousands of engineering hours, on Thanksgiving Day, 1965, a Coors production line was converted to draw and iron and yielded cans with a mirror finish. Despite thinner walls, they were stronger and more economical.

Success had finally been achieved. Recognizing the compatibility of the aluminum can with both beer and environment--and after realizing vital design and production breakthroughs--by November 12, 1971, Coors had completely converted from steel to aluminum cans. Coors' discovery of the suitability of aluminum for packaging, coupled with numerous technological breakthroughs, resulted in the formation of Coors Container Company in 1971. Today, the company's plant is the world's largest single plant devoted to making aluminum beer containers. It has become a prime example of the successful use of space-age technology, yielding a quality product at low cost--one that is desirable for both man and his environment. And, equally as impressive, the revolutionary new manufacturing techniques patented by Coors were shared with the rest of the brewing beverage and container manufacturing community. Moreover, Coors took a leadership role by initiating the nation's first consumer recycling program.

Coors Cash for Cans: An Instant Success

The "Coors Cash for Cans" recycling program, for any brand of used beer or soft drink beverage containers, was started in 1970. The program was a logical outgrowth of the company's conversion to aluminum and its commitment to minimize the environmental impact of its packaging materials. At Coors, the name of the family, the name of the products and the name of the company are all the same--"Coors." This fact prompted the company to be aggressive in its recycling activities, since the idea of having valuable aluminum cans tossed into the trash, or, worse yet, littered by the company's customers was unappealing to the company's family management. Further, the management realized that the entire brewing industry would do great disservice to itself unless it showed a greater responsibility for reducing litter and waste generated by its packaging materials. So, Coors started paying cash for aluminum beverage cans, and for Coors bottles, that were returned to public redemption centers which had been newly established by its distributors.

At first these centers were open on a limited basis, and the payout to the public was small (10 cents per pound for aluminum in 1970). However, environmentally concerned consumers, civic groups and individuals, who in the 1970s were to become "professional can recyclers" for the cash incentive, greeted Cash for Cans with enthusiasm. Their participation assured the program of instant success. The voluntary program started by Coors was copied by others in business and industry, but despite their participation Coors still recycles about one-third of all the aluminum recycled nationally. As a result of the company's leadership, many recyclers have remained loyal to Cash for Cans. Throughout the years the cash incentive has risen and today it stands at an average of 23 cents per pound for aluminum, the actual payout varying by area and promotional event.

When Bill Coors announced the formation of Cash for Cans, the distributors executed the program with great enthusiasm and dedication, despite the trials, inconvenience and expense of launching a pioneering effort.

COORS REVERSE DISTRIBUTION SYSTEM

Cash for Cans is an extensive program whose mechanics and benefits are spelled out in the next two sections.

Mechanics and Economics

The main element of this "reverse distribution system" is the organization by each Coors distributor of a recycling center on his property, as well as optional remote sites in his marketing area. Consumers bring any brand of beer or soft drink aluminum cans to the center, where Coors employees pay cash, based upon the net weight of the cans. The Coors distributor furnishes labor, utilities, supplies, some equipment, and possibly local transportation, as part of his agreement with the brewery to be aggressively involved in recycling. This agreement is covered in the contract between Adolph Coors Company and the distributor, but it allows him considerable flexibility as to degree of participation by the distributor. Since 1970, more than one-half billion pounds of cans have been recovered, and Coors distributors continue to apply the expertise gained in marketing Coors products to marketing recycling. The company uses every possible technique to increase the return rates of containers for recycling.

For their efforts in conducting and promoting the program, the distributors are reimbursed the price paid to the public, plus six-cents-per-pound compensation from Coors Container Company, which has the responsibility for disposition of the scrap. Coors Container's Recycling Department has the responsibility for recycling operations and for securing new metal supplies for the huge can-making plant. Flowing from a central department, communication with aluminum suppliers is almost constant, whether for discussions of metal purchases or for scrap recycling.

This approach has several advantages. It centralizes all communications with the company's vital metal suppliers, allows the company to rapidly and efficiently implement new programs or policies and integrates the brewery's efforts with that of its entire distributor organization.

But at the heart of the Coors recycling venture is an economic principle which gives Coors advantages over other aluminum users within its industry. In 1979, a staggering 100 million pounds of used aluminum cans will flow from Coors distributors' centers to aluminum companies. This immense poundage gives Coors leverage in its efforts to obtain new can stock at the best possible cost.

The combination of Cash for Cans scrap and manufacturing scrap generated within Coors Container allows Coors to return 80 percent of the metal it purchases. Economically, this is an unprecedented position for a brewer and is the direct result of the Cash for Cans campaign. Such a strong economic lever then opens up several business strategies.

Tolling is one of them. Coors has been successful in convincing Aluminum Company of America (Alcoa) to institute a program whereby scrap aluminum cans can be recycled into new sheet. Coors just pays Alcoa a service charge to process its scrap aluminum. There are financial advantages to this approach since Coors, as well as the aluminum companies, would otherwise be faced with generating expensive and energy-intensive primary aluminum rather than recycling scrap. Tolling means that Coors must pay a service charge or a conversion cost to replace a pound of its scrap with a pound of usable can sheet. Based on the price of scrap and the comparable cost of new sheet at full list price, tolling can represent a financial advantage to Coors.

Another possible strategy, whose opportunities and risks Coors has been evaluating, is to convert scrap aluminum by building its own aluminum melting and fabricating facility. In effect, Coors must compare the toll charge from Alcoa and other metal suppliers with the cost of converting scrap itself. A two-year analysis by Coors has brought it near a decision point, likely some time next year, on the prospects for self-manufacture of aluminum. The objective, in either the tolling program or the fabrication plant, would be to gain greater control over critical packaging material.

The objective of such control of metal costs is compatible with the company's overall philosophy of gaining, wherever possible, a remarkable degree of vertical integration. For example, Coors produces its own special barley seed, malts the barley at its own facilities, operates two rice milling facilities, designs most of its own machinery, constructs most of its own facilities, operates three gas- and coal-fired boilers, operates its own trucking fleet and so forth.

The metal management strategies of Coors Container are compatible with the business objectives of Coors Industries. One can see these strategies in sharp focus when considering that 60 percent of Coors barrelage cost is atrributed to packaging and 75 percent of its packaging is in aluminum cans! The ever-rising cost of aluminum has driven to 70 percent the metal portion of Coors can costs. Thus, any opportunity to control metal costs has a direct influence on packaging and barrelage costs and, ultimately, on the financial stability and condition of Coors Industries.

There Are More Payouts

Coors believes that obtaining and controlling scrap aluminum will serve at least two vital functions: It will maintain the company's leadership status with consumers, environmental and civic organizations, and it will maintain the company's bargaining power to keep aluminum costs as low as possible. But the marketing implications of Coors recycling commitment is subtle and not so easily measured.

One thing is certain: recycling is good P.R. Coors payment of money for the purchase of the empty beverage containers has allowed the company to demonstrate its goodwill toward its consumers and its willingness to be involved in community activities which serve a worthwhile purpose.

This P.R. value is apparent in the various techniques that Coors has used to gain greater participation in, and understanding for, the Cash for Cans program. The company has produced colored slide programs which its distributors show to school and civic groups. These programs tell of the benefits of recycling, Coors' commitment to environmental quality and, most importantly, provide information and motivation for viewers to take part in the recycling effort. Also, the company issues news releases to the media on a regular basis to report on the program's progress and to show Coors as a leader in this community service program. All of these communications tools have aided the company in "putting its best foot forward" with the general public, environmental activists, legislators, governmental agencies and the like. There's no question, the attention to recycling has benefited the company's image. While Coors gets the scrap back for recycling and a boosted image, the money paid out for the empties to individuals or groups helps them add to their income or raise money for the purchase of school supplies, philanthropic donations and endeavors of all kinds.

Studies show that most people recycle for the money. As one may expect, Coors recycling clientele is made up mostly from people on fixed incomes and from the minority communities where there is always a need for supplemental income. Every transaction for recycle cans--and there are hundreds of thousands of these each year--is an opportunity for Coors to portray a positive company image and to stimulate beer sales. These then are intrinsic values as a result of the presence of Coors redemption centers throughout the community. Additionally, Coors personnel have conducted on-the-spot marketing surveys and identified marketshare of leading brands of beer by the mix and volume of the empties collected by local consumers. These spot surveys, and the personal attention given to recyclers, do tend to aid distributors in their roles as community leaders. This attention to marketing surveys is but one part of Coors development of new, sophisticated--and expensive--sales, advertising, corporate communications and marketing programs designed to capture what the brewer calls, "the lion's share of the market." But packaging costs are critical to profitability. Through Cash for

Cans, the company has been able to work toward control of metal costs, which may in the long pull help fund the costly marketing efforts. Apparently, this same view is shared by Coors competitors, who are now beginning to expand their recycling efforts, too.

WHERE INDUSTRY STANDS TODAY

Many brewers have undertaken aggressive recycling campaigns in view of aluminum's economic power. Anheuser Busch, the nation's largest brewer, announced this year a broad recycling commitment with the intention of becoming a significant factor in the recovery of packaging materials, **primarily aluminum**. And aluminum companies themselves are also assuming a larger role in can recycling. This new aggressive posture of suppliers and competitors has confirmed the foresight of Coors officials. Considering the fate of the aluminum can at stake, over a decade ago management had the company take an assertive position on consumer recycling, notwithstanding at that time the restrained enthusiasm of suppliers and competitors. Today their renewed interest is welcomed by Coors. But to compete for the recycling business--namely, recovery of 75 percent of the aluminum that existing program techniques still leave uncovered today--the industry must provide greater convenience to consumers who want to turn in cans. In 1979 that percentage amounted to 1.2 billion pounds of scrap cans.

IS RESOURCE RECOVERY THE ANSWER?

The immense quantity of valuable can scrap just mentioned ended up either as uncollected litter or as an important contribution to the solid waste stream of the country. Coors sees waste resource recovery as a business and engineering concept. It will surely be required to lessen the demand on landfills and to generate new sources of energy by the burning of trash combustibles. Unfortunately, given present technology, once used aluminum cans are discarded as trash, the possibility of contamination is so great that recovered aluminum for food packaging seems impractical.

The Cash for Cans program, however, is truly a closed loop system. Used cans are converted to new can sheet, thereby reducing energy costs and conserving depletable natural resources. There is a legitimate 95 percent energy savings in using scrap aluminum versus the production of primary aluminum from bauxite. Bauxite, from which aluminum is initially made, is largely imported from outside the U.S., so balance-of-trade considerations also come into play.

A number of states have adopted deposit legislation to encourage the return of empty beverage containers. This remains as another popular resource recovery technique.

COORS' POSITION ON DEPOSIT LEGISLATION

Coors is opposed to deposit legislation. It is particularly opposed to legislation which places different deposit values on cans and bottles. In fact, a discriminatory deposit at the state or local level would be disastrous for the beverage industry. What Coors has been advocating--at some professional risk for its competitors--is for the entire industry to join forces in a broad-based voluntary recycling effort. Contrasted with this approach would be to have legislators, who sometimes are uninformed about beverage distribution and economic consequences, mandate laws that could be disruptive and costly to the packaging, brewing and bottling industries.

Despite its opposition to deposits, Coors cannot ignore the possibility of this legislation in some of its markets. In fact, Coors will be selling its products in Iowa this year under a uniform five-cent deposit law. In developing a strategy to accommodate deposits, Coors has devised an approach which attempts to deal with conservation objectives as seen by environmentalists, as well as with the practical aspects of the reverse distribution of great volumes of used packaging materials. To make the economics of a deposit system work, Coors has drawn on its experience in the Cash for Cans program, from which it has learned the importance of materials management. For example, improper attention to the details of scrap handling, transportation and financial management could very well lead to higher beverage costs for the consumer, a drop in sales and changes in the package mix. The issue for deposits rests on what costs and inconveniences are associated with the highly desirable goals of reducing litter, energy consumption and solid waste.

If deposit legislation is implemented, the amount of the deposit should be uniform for cans and bottles. Also, such legislation should be implemented at the federal level, superseding state and local legislation, which represents a patchwork of regulations leading directly to higher costs for compliance.

In its view of a deposit system, Coors sees the need for empty cans to be crushed at the earliest point in the return cycle so they cannot be illegally returned again. Also, handling the empties as you would full cans being distributed to retailers is prohibitively costly. Regretfully, most deposit laws do not allow for the crushing and mixing of cans by brand for ultimate separation on a weight basis. This stipulation is necessary to keep costs at a reasonable level for the return and recycling of the used containers.

To be tolerable, a deposit law should have an additional stipulation. Unrefunded deposit money should be used to help underwrite the processing and transportation costs of cans and the administrative costs of the return cycle. This way, a person who forfeits the deposit amount by throwing away a deposit container indirectly contributes money to a pool of funds used to recover and process the returning empties.

THE DEPARTMENT OF ENERGY PROGRAM FOR THE RECOVERY
OF ENERGY AND MATERIALS FROM URBAN WASTE

Donald K. Walter
Urban Waste and Municipal Systems Branch
Office of Buildings and Community Systems
U.S. Department of Energy

INTRODUCTION

Municipal solid waste -- the discards of society or "garbage" if you will -- is a valuable commodity. It contains energy. As such, solid waste has a new, and deserved, respectability.

Historically, society has treated solid waste as a "problem." The public attitude has been more or less to rid ourselves of it as quickly and cheaply as possible. This attitude is understandable in the context of history. Until recently, fossil fuels were still believed cheap and abundant. Although the energy in waste material could be recovered, there was no compelling need to do so.

Time, economics, and social need have forced reevaluation of our attitudes. Today solid waste is not a problem to be rid of; it is an opportunity to produce energy and reduce our reliance on scarce fossil fuels. In the midst of the energy crisis, solid waste is an asset.

This year alone we will discard approximately 180 million tons of municipal solid waste. If it were all recovered, it could supply approximately two percent of our total energy needs by directly replacing nonrenewable fossil fuels. Further, the inorganics, such as aluminum, steel and glass, if recovered and recycled, would reduce the amount of energy required to produce these materials by an additional one percent of our total energy use. While seemingly small, it should be remembered that this energy source is currently discarded as having no use. As a means of displacing or reducing the use of nonrenewable fuels, these figures are no small contribution.

Since past technical developments aimed at the large system, only sixty percent of today's waste stream is recoverable. Our goal is to increase that figure. The U.S. Department of Energy (DOE) -- recognizing the potential of municipal waste as well as the wastes from our industrial, agricultural and forestry environs as valuable sources of energy -- has instituted programs in each area. The purpose here is to describe briefly the DOE municipal waste-to-energy program.

The primary mission of the Urban Waste and Municipal Systems Branch (UWMS) of the Department of Energy is to promote the widespread use of the urban waste as a source of energy and materials. The program is a broad-based one and does not confine itself solely to urban waste. Other elements include developing methods that will reduce the amount of energy consumed in carrying out essential local governmental services such as wastewater treatment.

While important, the potential to displace fossil energy of the "municipal systems" portion of the Urban Waste and Municipal Systems Branch is only one-half that of the "urban waste" portion. For this reason I would like to concentrate on urban waste activities which are grouped into the following areas: technical processes, institutional impediments to waste use, and program (monetary) support.

TECHNICAL PROCESSES

The technical processes associated with energy and materials recovery from urban waste fall into three broad categories: mechanical, thermal, and biological. These technologies can be ranked according to their stage of development as shown in Table 1. The technologies require good organization and central waste recovery activities. The recovery of energy and materials from waste in centralized plants is still in the early stages of commercial development. As already mentioned, our technology has been developed to the point where sixty percent of our waste stream can be recovered, but in 1978 less than one percent of the nation's total urban waste stream was actually recovered. The reason for this low figure is that the necessary technologies are in the early stages of development. Plants now beginning commercial operation still need operating histories to document technical and economic feasibility. Fig. 1 shows the range of application of the mechanical, thermal, and biological processes.

Mechanical

Mechanical processing separates wastes into various components including metals, glass, and a refuse-derived fuel (RDF). Generally, a mechanical process is a preliminary step to the thermal and biological technologies which convert the organics to energy. The metal, glass, and paper fibers are recycled to displace virgin materials.

Mechanical processes have two basic functions: homogenization and separation. A typical processing line will use a screen for size separation and shredding for size reduction or

TABLE 1

DEVELOPMENTAL STAGE OF RESOURCE RECOVERY TECHNOLOGIES

Level of Development	Technology
High	• Ferrous Metal Recovery
	• Anaerobic Digestion of Municipal Liquid Wastes
	• Wasterwall and Modular Controlled Air Combustors
	• Coarse, Fluff, and Wet Pulped RDF
	• Paper Fiber Recovery
	• Landfill Gas Recovery
	• Glass, Aluminum and Other Nonferrous Metal Recovery
	• Dust and Densified RDF
	• Pyrolysis and Gasifiers
	• Anaerobic Digestion of Solid Waste
Low	• Enzymatic and Fungal Synthesis

FIGURE I TECHNICAL PROCESSES

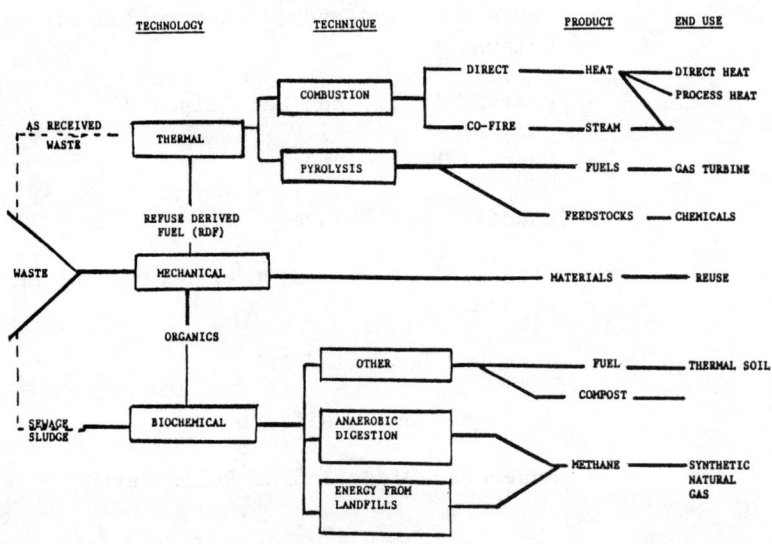

homogenization of raw refuse. This is followed by some form of air classification that separates the particles into light (organics) and heavy (inorganics) material streams. The light fraction has come to be known as fluff RDF. Its use is principally as a fuel, either in a specially designed boiler or in conjunction with coal in an existing boiler.

There is one facility now operating that recovers and uses fluff RDF on a daily basis, but it has encountered a series of economic and technical problems. A second facility is entering its first year of production evaluation prior to completion of fuel sales contracts. Several other facilities are under construction or undergoing testing prior to beginning commercial operation.

Fluff RDF can be further improved by turning it into RDF through pelletizing, briquetting, or extruding. This produces a denser fuel that is more easily transported and stored. It is particularly adapted for stoker and spreader-stoker furnaces. However, it has not been demonstrated commercially, and the costs, handling characteristics, and firing characteristics remain to be evaluated. The anticipated advantages of densified RDF are an enhanced energy content per unit weight and improved storage and transportation characteristics.

The production of powder RDF (particles smaller than 0.15 millimeter) is being developed by means of a proprietary pilot-plant process. After adding an embrittling chemical, coarsely shredded waste is pulverized to a dust-like consistency. The resulting powder RDF has a higher Btu content than fluff RDF, along with greater density, homogeneity, and decreased moisture content. In addition, powder RDF may be capable of direct cofiring with fuel oils. However, the dust-like composition creates a need for special handling to minimize the danger of an explosion.

A "wet" mechanical separation process uses hydropulping technology adapted from the pulp and paper industry to reduce raw waste to a more uniform size and consistency, followed by a centrifugal, liquid cycle process for separating the pulped mass into light and heavy fractions.

Ferrous metal recovery systems are the most advanced material recovery systems. Paper fiber recovery, by both wet pulping and dry processes, and aluminum and glass recovery have been tested with limited success. Efforts are planned to improve system efficiencies in terms of energy use, quantity, and quality of material recovered.

Thermal

Combustion techniques burn waste for the recovery of heat energy. Waterwall combustors are the most technically developed systems and employ special grates to burn urban waste "as received" and to recover steam either at saturated or superheated conditions. Over 250 plants are operating in Europe and Japan. There are seven plants operating in the United States. Three of these were originally constructed as incinerators and only recently obtained energy markets. Worldwide, there have been a number of technical problems in waterwall combustors with the control of corrosion and erosion being the most serious. The most recent European designs have solved these problems but at an increased capital cost.

The more popular U.S. development seems to be the recovery of RDF for sale to coal-using facilities. With modifications, existing boilers can use RDF as a supplemental fuel. Most development has been aimed at the large suspension-fired utility boiler and, while test burns have been encouraging, technical problems have developed. These are related to burning characteristics, slagging, and the performance of environmental control equipment. All can be solved. However, upgrading control devices such as electrostatic precipitators may require significant increases in the capital costs of systems using RDF as a supplemental fuel.

Another variation being demonstrated is the combustion of RDF as a principal fuel in a dedicated boiler. Normally, the boiler is of spreader-stoker design with some consideration given to the use of fossil fuels -- such as high sulfur coal as a load leveler and steam production stabilizer.

The only available small-scale system is a packaged two-chamber incinerator with waste heat recovery. This technique is practical at the scale of 25 to 100 tons per day (TPD). Partial oxidation occurs in the first section of the unit and causes a portion of the waste material to degrade and give off combustible gases. These gases, as well as products of combustion and particulates from the first chamber, flow to a second chamber where they are combusted with excess air and a natural gas or oil pilot flame. The combustion products then flow through appropriate heat transfer equipment to produce steam, hot water, or hot air. Today five small cities and more than sixty industrial plants use the technique with heat recovery equipment.

Thermal gasification and pyrolysis systems are also under development with several systems approaching the full-scale demonstration stage. Fuels from these processes include gases, liquids, and chars.

Biological

Biological techniques use living organisms to convert organics into useful energy forms. These processes are in the developmental stages. DOE is sponsoring an anaerobic digestion process that converts the organics in urban waste to methane under controlled conditions. This process is at the proof-of-concept stage and is not expected to be commercial until the late 1980s.

Sanitary landfills naturally degrade and produce a mixture of methane and carbon dioxide. Because of the explosive nature of the gas, early work considered only migration control. Subsequently, the use of the gas for energy purposes was recognized. Today there are several sites in operation or under development to recover the gas and use it for boiler fuel or for injection into natural gas pipelines. It is estimated that one trillion cubic feet of methane is potentially recoverable from existing landfills with 33 billion cubic feet of pipeline-quality methane available yearly just from the 100 largest landfills.

The preceeding was a brief description of the technical options to recover energy or materials from wastes. As noted, these are in varying stages of development. Overall, waste-to-energy constitutes an emerging technology in the early stages of development. At best, the experience has been spotty. Plants have not performed up to early expectations, although as time passes, the technological problems are being solved through plant modifications or by modifying operation and maintenance procedures. From the DOE viewpoint, perhaps the principal concern is that plants have been constructed as waste disposers, not energy producers. These institutional issues are as inhibiting to the success of waste-to-energy plants as are technological concerns.

NON-TECHNICAL IMPEDIMENTS

Figure 2 illustrates the range of nontechnical issues in resource recovery. The three broad categories -- institutional, socioeconomic, and legal -- are interrelated and often raise obstacles more difficult to overcome than technical problems.

Institutional problems related to producing energy from urban waste are complex. For example, local governments, which usually collect and dispose of a large fraction of urban waste, view resource recovery systems as exotic and expensive methods of waste disposal. Consequently, most local governments have little inclincation or incentive to pioneer in waste recovery

FIGURE 2 NONTECHNICAL ISSUES AND THEIR INTERRELATIONSHIPS

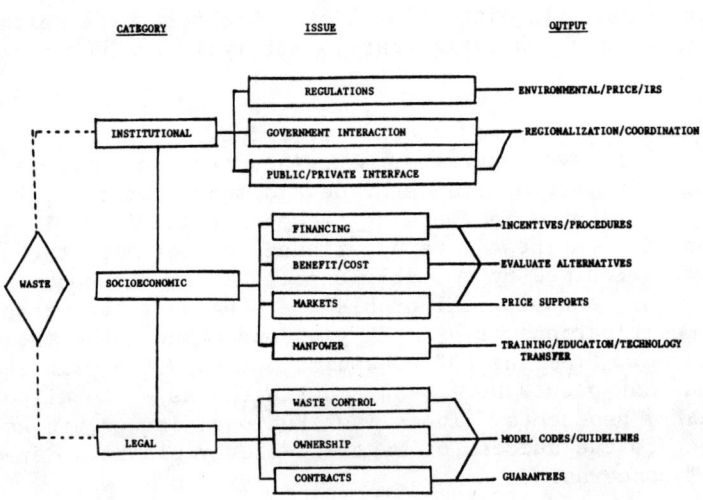

technology. They wish only to dispose of the waste as painlessly and inexpensively as possible. The growing pinch in energy supplies and the increasing cost of waste disposal are slowly overcoming the reluctance of local governments to use resource recovery. Nevertheless, serious problems still exist. These include local government authority to mandate disposal methods, the inability to assure adequate waste supplies to an energy-producing resource recovery facility, and the difficulty in obtaining intergovernmental cooperation for support of metropolitan or regional resource recovery facilities.

To be economically viable, waste-to-energy plants depend on two major sources of income: the sale of the energy product and a fee to dispose of waste in the plant (tipping fee). Additional income can be realized from the sale of recovered materials. Where landfill (tipping fees) or energy costs are high, waste-based systems can compete with fossil fuels.

The perception of waste as a disposal problem and the desire to construct resource recovery systems only if they are competitive with other disposal methods (such as sanitary landfill) present a major obstacle. If excess processing capacity is built in a plant, the added cost can be capitalized only by increased unit tipping fees or increased selling prices of energy products. Further, when plant economics are reviewed realistically and the energy sales price is set at market value, then the tipping fee in most areas exceeds the cost of landfills. However, when life cycle costs are traced, then the project is indeed economic.

The difficulty in demonstrating that resource recovery systems can be economically attractive creates yet another problem: local governments are adverse to accepting the financial and technical risks such projects present. As a result, several innovative approaches to project financing are being developed that spread the risks, and potential rewards, among all resource recovery participants. These financing approaches are beneficial because they force project sponsors to do several things. Sponsors have to thoroughly investigate the anticipated performance of proposed recovery systems; assure that project revenues are both secured and sufficient to cover all operating and debt service costs; and assess and allocate risks.

DOE activities in the nontechnical area include the assessment of economic, social, institutional and legal barriers to resource recovery, and development and demonstration of generic, innovative solutions. We have in place a Memorandum of Understanding with the Environmental Protection Agency (EPA). It assigns EPA responsibility for the support of feasibility and procurement planning studies, thus drawing on the Agency's past experience with solid waste management planning. DOE will support the design and construction of plants, thus insuring that local systems are implemented with energy recovery as the motivation.

DOE's nontechnical program also includes evaluation of public attitudes and institutional barriers to resource recovery; also benefit/cost studies that evaluate the social costs of resource recovery and disposal options, including the cost of environmental damages and external factors such as the balance of payments and national defense. In addition, the program includes development of methods that will properly compare resource recovery with traditional waste disposal options and methods for estimating the life cycle costs of resource recovery systems.

These efforts are being augmented by a diversified program of economic incentives, consisting of grants, contracts, cooperative agreements, loans, loan guarantees, and price supports for demonstration plants. Both loan guarantee and price support regulations are being developed, but no appropriations are available for these programs. An active program of training, technical assistance, and information transfer is also being initiated. This includes preparation of case studies, conducting workshops and seminars, and developing university and apprenticeship programs. And lastly, the program is being coordinated among the Federal agencies so that the expertise of each is used to the fullest. Overall, each of these efforts was shaped by DOE's belief that resource recovery from municipal waste is far too important for any artificially contrived impediment to be tolerated.

Waste-to-energy technology is the only method of waste disposal that simultaneously achieves two important public goals: it produces an alternative fuel that reduces our dependence on fossil fuel, and it disposes of our ever increasing amounts of solid waste in an environmentally acceptable manner. The ability of urban waste technology to accomplish both makes it more than one disposal option among many -- it is an imperative.

What can the consumer do? Be aware that municipal waste is an opportunity to be exploited for its energy content. Even though there are technical and institutional problems, they can be overcome. Where appropriate, the consumer should work for the creation of facilities but understand that development is difficult and lengthy. Find the strong individual that in almost any successful project seems to be the guiding light. Ask the important questions of how much, how long, whose risk, and so forth. But recognize definitely that the key idea is to view municipal waste as an asset and as an underutilized resource. Seek system development not simply as a disposal option, but rather as an opportunity for a new energy and material resource.

BIBLIOGRAPHY

Ahlstrom, S.B., and R.R. Spencer (1978), <u>Assessment of Powdered Activated Carbon Addition to Anaerobic Digestion at Salt Lake City, Utah</u>, Richland, WA., Pacific Northwest Laboratory

<u>Department of Energy Authorization Act of 1978 -- Civilian Applications</u> (1978), Public Law 95-238 (February).

Department of Energy (Urban Waste Technology Branch) and DSI Resource Systems Group, unpublished planning document, Argonne National Laboratory and Boston, Mass.

Department of Energy (1978), "Proceedings of Symposium on the Utilization of Methane Generated in Landfills," The John Hopkins University (March).

<u>European Waste-to-Energy Systems</u>: An Overview (1977), National Technical Information Service Document Number: CONS/2103-6 (June).

<u>Federal Nonnuclear Research and Development Act of 1974</u> (1974), Public Law 95-577 (December).

Kirkland, D.R., et.al., (1978), <u>Summary of 1977 Fiscal Year Efforts to Establish Test Procedures for the Determination of the Gross Calorific Value of Refuse and Refuse-Derived-Fuels by Oxygen Bomb Calorimetry</u>, Draft Report, National Bureau of Standards.

Los Angeles County Sanitary District (1978), "Proposed Delivery of Puente Hills Landfill Gas to Rio Hondo College," proposal submitted to the DOE in response to PRDA #EM-78-D-01-5153 (August).

Mitre Corporation (1975), <u>Energy Conservation Waste Utilization Research and Development Plan</u> (July).

New York State Energy Research and Development Authority (1978), "Landfill Gas-to-Electric Conversion Project," proposal submitted in response to PRDA #EM-78-D-01-5153 (August).

Pacific Gas and Electric Company (1978), "Utilization of Landfill Gas from City of Mountain View," proposal submitted to the DOE in response to PRDA #EM78-D-01-5153 (August).

Pfeffer, J.T., and J.C. Liebman (1976a) "Energy from Refuse by Bioconversion, Fermentation, and Residue Disposal Processes," Resource Recovery and Conservation, Vol. 1, 295-313.

Pfeffer, J.T., and J.C. Liebman (1976b), "Biological Conversion of Organic Refuse to Methane," Final Report No. ERDA/NSR/RANN/AER 73-07872/FR/76/4, Vol. 1 and 2, University of Illinois (November).

Resource Conservation and Recovery Act of 1976 (1976), Public Law 94-580, (October).

Spano, L.A., Enzymatic Hydrolysis of Cellulose to Glucose, Quarterly Reports, U.S. Army Natick Research and Development Command, Natick, Mass.

United States Environmental Protection Agency (Office of Solid Waste Management Programs) (1974a), Report to Congress, First Report.

_____ (1974b), Report to Congress, Second Report.

_____ (1975), Report to Congress, Third Report

_____ (1977), Report to Congress, Fourth Report

Walter, Donald K., C. Rines and S. Levy (1978), Commercialization Strategy Report for Energy from Urban Wastes, Document Number TID-28852.

Waste Management, Inc. RefCOM-Status Report Covering the Start-up Phase, March 15 - October 1978, F.

CAUSES, CONTROL, AND CONFUSIONS

W. J. Coppoc, Texaco Inc.

INTRODUCTION

Bertrand Russell once said, "Men desire to be in control because they are afraid that the control of others will be used unjustly to their detriment." The United States Constitution placed rather broad responsibilities -- and opportunities -- for control on the Congress. They are set forth in the form of powers delineated in Section 8 of Article I of the U.S. Constitution. After 200 years this remarkable section still makes most interesting reading.

Much has been said for a long time, but particularly in very recent years, about the tremendous burden of regulation which is borne by the American people under various laws passed at various times. Many statements have been emphasizing both the inhibiting effect of those regulations and the beneficial effect their proponents claim these regulations have brought to the country.

On Table 1, I have listed just a few of the "causes" which have been popular in the United States since the American Revolution in more or less chronological order. First we worried about unification of the colonies and their defense, the raising of an army, etc.; then we were presented with the problems of the frontier, its protection, and its expansion. Then slavery; then unity again; then the problems of expansion, which brought worries about monopoly; then we had a flurry of isms, including McCarthyism. Then we were concerned with the poor, and our struggles to eliminate poverty; the Civil Rights movement; environmental causes; and now energy. I make no pretense that this is a complete list but it is representative of various causes -- deserving our consideration -- which have flourished in the United States and which have drawn large numbers of people to carry their banners.

TABLE 1

CAUSES

Unification	Monopoly
Defense	Isms
The Frontier	Poverty
Slavery	Civil Rights
Unity	Environment
Expansion	Energy

CAUSES: POLITICAL NATURE AND RESULTS

Causes have certain characteristics worthy of study. The first is that causes as such are the necessary grist for the politician's mill. Without a cause a politician has little chance of unseating an opponent, or remaining in office himself -- unless he has an organization in his home district so strong that it stifles all opposition. I have never forgotten a quote once attributed to a leading senator by a rather well-known academician who consulted, frequently and over many years, with members of Congress and of successive administrations. The academician told me he had put the following question to the senator, who was quite conservative: "How do you decide which causes to promote?" To his surprise, the senator replied, "The principal requisite is that it has to cost a lot of money. If a cause doesn't cost a lot of money, it's not going to get much attention, either from the Congress or from the people generally."

So if a "cause" generates a lot of popular discussion, commands a great deal of attention from the news media, generally seems to be creating considerable excitement among the populace -- and involves a lot of money -- we can depend on its being picked up by a politician somewhere and promptly made into a "cause celebre".

The path of events is then fairly predictable. The politician will view with alarm. The terrible consequences which he claims would descend upon the country if "something isn't done" will command headlines and lead news stories across the country. Since "something has to be done" something will be done and controls of one sort or another will be enacted. Since the purpose of the controls is to control, it means that there will be a reduction in freedom of action imposed upon some portion of the population and, very probably, on the economy.

Another way of stating this point is that the people have recognized a collective responsibility and have moved to discharge that responsibility in democratic fashion through the enactment of laws and regulations.

In Table 2, I have indicated what happens as a result of highly publicizing a cause. Reaction to the cause is control and the result of the control is a reduction of individual freedom. Also, a reduction of individual responsibility for self.

TABLE 2

REACTION TO CAUSES

Recognition of (or Assumption of) Collective Responsibility for Causes and People
Reaction Controls
1. <u>Reduction</u> of Individual Freedom
2. <u>Reduction</u> of Individual Responsibility for Self
3. <u>Increase</u> of Individual Responsibility for Others and for Common-Use Things^a
^a Item 3 is Generally Exercised Collectively

Controls also result in the increase of individual responsibility for others and for common-use things. Interestingly, and in a sense oddly enough, number three on the diagram is generally exercised collectively. This means that taxes, direct or indirect, are assessed and the immediate <u>working</u> responsibility for others or for common-use things is placed upon people who are compensated for discharging this collective responsibility; and the <u>individual</u> part of the responsibility as it applies to the ordinary citizen frequently consists only of paying those taxes.

Some of the things that happened as a result of the causes in our list are shown in Table 3. Our "unification" cause resulted in The Declaration of Independence, Articles of Confederation, and finally The Constitution. The need for "defense" resulted in conscription -- and in taxes. Among other things the "frontier" cause resulted in The Homestead Act, etc., "slavery" in abolition, "unity" in the Civil War and reconstruction, "expansion" in antisweat shop regulations, etc., "monopoly" in anti-trust laws, "isms" in restriction of political beliefs -- recall the declaration that had to be signed during World War II and after if one were involved in any secret activities or required clearance of any sort -- the cause for "poverty" resulted in social security provisions and welfare plans. Our "civil rights" cause, which produced educational, employment, compensation, and business practices which were strange to us, actually changed interpersonal ways of life. The "environmental" cause resulted in regulations and standards for air, water, solid wastes, and toxic materials and a host of direct and indirect regulations; and the concern for "energy" resulted in price and distribution controls on energy raw materials, subsidies of different activities, and an intricate complex of regulatory legislation and actions.

TABLE 3

CAUSES AND THEIR RESULTS

Unification	-	Declaration of Independence, Articles of Confederation, The Constitution
Defense	-	Conscription, Taxes
The Frontier	-	Homestead Act
Slavery	-	Abolition
Unity	-	Civil War and Reconstruction
Expansion	-	Anti-Sweatshop Regulations, Etc.
Monopoly	-	Anti-Trust Laws
Isms	-	Restriction of Political Beliefs
Poverty	-	Social Security, Welfare Plans
Civil Rights	-	Educational, Employment, Compensation, and Business Practices
Environment	-	Air, Water, Solid Waste, Toxics Standards
Energy	-	Price and Distribution Controls, Subsidies, Etc.

The overall results of these laws and regulations, imposed over essentially two hundred years, have been that freedom of individual action has been reduced, personal interactions quite seriously altered, and in many cases considerable benefits have been obtained. One wonders, for example, what would have happened had the people as a whole, in the form of government, not stepped in to control the excesses which were unquestionably being committed in many areas of public and private life. Unrestrained activity in any field almost automatically results in excesses which eventually prove detrimental to the interests of all people, both individually and collectively. (Obviously the objective of many laws has been to protect individual freedom -- and these constitute a very interesting case study in themselves.)

REGULATION, EXCESS HARM HERE, TOO

That unrestrained regulatory activity is similarly detrimental is a conclusion to which one jumps almost automatically. But what are the detrimental effects of excessive regulation? Aside from the mountains of paperwork and the out-of-pocket costs of maintaining large staffs of regulators, what are the detrimental effects of well-intentioned but excessive regulation?

Time will permit only a quick mention of some of the detriments. Possibly the greatest detriment -- and quite unquantifiable -- is the inhibiting effect on positive business decisions and on innovative activity. Regulation reduces individual responsibility in the regulated field and replaces it with mandated rigidity which, without exception in my experience, introduces inequities. In an attempt to remove the inequities, a modified regulation is imposed. Usually this modified regulation is more complex and requires more staff -- and more lawyers. All of which, in addition to reducing individual responsibility, increases the uncertainties of a venture, the business risk involved, and the probability that a responsible business management will reject a proposal in the regulated field. This inhibiting effect is a most significant factor which, in my opinion, is responsible for a large part of the economic problems the United States has faced in the last decade. No small factor in these problems has been the mandated diversion of resources of all kinds from economically productive to economically unproductive uses.

A real hazard which results from intensive regulation and the requisite large staffs is that the regulators tend to become powerful advocates. They are apt to approach a scientific or economic problem with a preconceived solution, as in an advocacy case, instead of with the objective analysis we expected from government agencies two or three decades ago.

A current example of this sort of thing is the series of reports[1] which have been issuing annually from the Council on Environmental Quality (e.g. 1977) and the Environmental Protection Agency (e.g. 1979) on the costs of environmental regulation. These reports have ignored all indirect costs and have consistently considered only the costs of installing, operating, and maintaining control hardware. Thus they have totally ignored the economic effects of such things as a four-year delay in the Alaska pipeline, the cancellation of two large chemical plants in the San Francisco Bay Area, the delay in construction of a refinery in tidewater Virginia, and a host of other less highly publicized delays and cancellations.

A most bothersome question is whether the benefits in these cases have actually been worth the loss in initiative, the loss in individual responsibility, and the diversion of effort and resources to unproductive activities. In other words, we have the old cost-benefit problem in front of us again.

EXAMPLES OF PROBLEMS CREATED BY CAUSES AND THEIR RESULTS

Of course, it is not my purpose to analyze each regulation. Instead let's examine several causes and their results that should merit consideration by people concerned with marketing principles and, in particular, people concerned with ecological marketing.

In the first place this group gathered here is concerned primarily with efforts to achieve necessary corrections of recognized problems through greater use of the marketplace rather than through greater use of governmentally imposed regulations. If I understand correctly, your general thesis is that one does not deny the existence of problems. One simply attempts to achieve more solutions within the scope of the incentives, checks, and balances which exist in the free interchange of goods and services.

We now turn to a closer examination of several of the causes listed in Table 3, searching for common threads to

---

[1] See Chase Econometric Associates, Inc. reports: "The Macroeconomic Impacts of Federal Pollution Control Programs," for 1975, 1976, and 1977. Also, Data Resources, Inc., report, "The Macroeconomic Impact of Federal Pollution Control Programs: 1978 Assessment," January 1979.

problems that have generally arisen in the wake of governmental action and results precipitated by the causes.

Social Security

Poverty is a cause one of whose chief results is Social Security. And it has a problem: The system could go bankrupt. One wonders how Congress could enact regulations which would result in the bankruptcy of a system which Congressmen themselves instituted. And of course to understand this, one has to understand that the budgeting process which existed in the United States up until 1977 was not at all a budgeting process in the sense that most of us understand. It was simply a listing of the anticipated expenditures. In the case of the Social Security actions no hard-nosed, objective analysis of income and outflow had been conducted <u>prior to the time</u> the Congress was asked to vote. This was a perfect case of single-minded pursuit of a single objective with insufficient consideration of the total picture.

Civil Rights

Next consider Civil Rights. A major problem the business community must face, as a consequence of the legislative results of this cause, is that the majority of personnel decisions now must be made on bases other than the evaluation of an individual's ability to perform in a particular position. Yet the opposite criterion -- ability to perform -- is what the efficiency of our entire system for supplying goods and services to the people of the country largely depends upon. Here again, we have a single-minded pursuit of a single objective with inadequate hard-nosed, objective consideration of exactly what the results would be.

Environmental Control

In the case of environmental control, I need hardly expand any more than to say that in this case, by congressional action, consideration of goals other than the health of the people was specifically forbidden in several cases.

Cost-benefit analyses in the environmental field have been performed ad infinitum. Once I told colleagues on a particular national committee that we could pretty well define the costs of controlling a particular effluent to a particular level, but that it was virtually impossible to define the benefits to be obtained from such control. That was before the enactment of such extensions to our environmental control regulations as the concept of nondeterioration, the regulations which apply in nonattainment areas, as well as various requirements for actions in perpetuity. It is these latter regulations which have resulted in the cancellation of the construction of large manufacturing facilities and the delay in the construction of the terminal facilities in Long Beach, California, for the transport of Alaskan crude to the Midwest. Again, our principal problem in connection with the environmental enactments has been a failure to conduct a hard-nosed, objective analysis of just what the results of a particular action would be in totality.

Energy

In the field of energy we have managed to place ourselves in hostage to the oil-producing nations of the world through a succession of actions beginning with price controls in 1971 or possibly with the so-called Phillips decision of 1954. Washington's insistence in 1973 that the price of domestically produced crude should be controlled at a level considerably below the world price of crude has resulted in a complex of regulatory actions that sound totally foreign to the United States. In fact many of my friends outside of the oil business to whom I have described the regulations of the so-called entitlements program established in November 1974, insist, even as of May, 1979, that "this can't happen here." Again, we have an example of regulations having been enacted without the hard-nosed, objective analysis of what their overall results would actually be.

OBJECTIVE ANALYSIS -- WHY IT IS LACKING?

Why is it that the "hard-nosed, objective analysis" I have been talking about is not routinely a part of all legislative and regulatory action? There are a number of reasons. One derives from the laudable concept of preventing "conflict of interest". The result has been rules and regulations so stringent that anyone who has real knowledge in a particular field, gained from long years of experience in either the public or private sector, is frequently excluded from government councils taking action within that field. A second reason is the extension of "standing" before the law. It has been extended to the point that individuals and groups with only the flimsiest of connections with a particular action can bring court actions which totally stymie projects of great national importance. Such people need have absolutely no responsibility for the project, no financial interest in it, but only a statement to the effect that it will affect them in some fashion. Again, this extension of the concept of "standing" before the law has been expanded with the best of motivation, but without hard-nosed, objective consideration to where it could lead.

THE MARKETPLACE, STRENGTHS, WEAKNESSES:
SUGGESTIONS, QUESTIONS AND ANSWERS

The marketplace is certainly the arena in which the largest number of different forces are brought to bear upon a particular problem in economics. I would not argue that it considers them all at any one time; but it certainly considers more of them simultaneously than would any small group of men and women assembled in a conference room in some center of government. Certainly the voters in the marketplace cast their ballots daily in favor of the product or company that they think provides the most quality and service for the price paid.

However, the marketplace suffers from serious deficiencies when it encounters problems that are social in nature; are not directly connected with the costs of production and distribution; and impose a competitive disadvantage upon a marketer who chooses to incur significant financial liability in an attempt to ameliorate such problems by action in the marketplace. Frequent remedies are environmental controls and efforts to correct employment inequities or to make ethnic ratios in a work force meet a predetermined number. For this reason, we frequently find businessmen calling upon government to establish regulations in order that all competitors will be saddled with equivalent costs for the proposed social benefit.

Nevertheless, many old problems remain and we can rest assured that new problems of this type will develop. Now would be a good time for me to propose to you the total solution. But I can't because I don't have a complete solution. I can, however, suggest that those who participate in the marketplace and know it best could very well increase their efforts along two particular lines, neither of which is new or unique.

The first of these lines is the age-old one of increasing the amount of statesmanlike conduct exhibited by the participants in the marketplace. During my career it has been a privilege to know quite a large number of leaders in the fields of politics, business, academia, and other learned professions. No one of these groups has a corner on statesmen, nor a corner on scalawags. But I've always been rather proud of the fact that, at least in my experience, business leaders rank just as high in "social consciousness quotient" as any of the others, and frequently exhibit a much more balanced and realistic appraisal of the sociological problems involved.

Groups of corporate executives have talked about the advisability of including in every rising young executive's training a good practical course in social responsibility. I think it is mandatory that those making appointments to high positions in any corporation not only provide for such social education in the background of the candidates, but closely examine the degree to which they exhibit social consciousness in the daily discharge of their responsibilities -- corporate and otherwise. American business must demonstrate this quality in the marketplace, and must not be bashful in properly calling attention to its performance, or it will continue to be vilified by the news media and defeated at the polls by politicians happy to exploit its silence.

The second line along which I strongly suggest improvement, and along which there has already been much improvement in recent years, is in the relationships between the practitioners in the marketplace and their elected representatives. That is, the degree to which businessmen actually participate in the political process in general.

I don't mean only electioneering. Politicians need help in making their decisions, and in most cases they know they need help and they welcome comments and advice by knowledgeable people. Show me another group of people who have to publicly cast a "yes" or "no" vote on such a wide variety of issues every week. Too frequently it seems to me we in the business world tend to sit outside of the political arena and confine our efforts to caustic criticism of those who choose to participate in that arena. I do not believe in two sets of values -- one for the public sector and one for the private sector -- in any area, whether it be economics, or ethics, or morals, or sociological thinking. If we in business are to be participants in the business of the country, we have to be sure that the business of the country includes an interest in the political participants upon whom we place the responsibility for much of what happens in the country.

Like it or not, we are no longer a frontier society. Our politicians can neither be elected nor re-elected if they exhibit only frontier thinking. Neither can American business expect wise business decisions from American politicians if individuals in business do not accept as a continuing obligation a responsibility to share their business expertise and their down-to-earth knowledge of the marketplace with their elected representatives.

Include all social costs in the price of the product? I frankly don't think it will work on a completely voluntary basis. Many "social" costs are already in the product price; Social Security, for example, and medical and retirement plans financed in whole or in part by the entrepreneur. But these are not usually altogether voluntary.

Maintain socially responsible statesmanship in marketplace behavior and constructive participation by business in political decisions? I can see nothing to prevent reaching such aims except social unconcern -- which American business now can simply ill-afford.

SAVE A TREE BAGS:
THE MARKETING OF AN ECOLOGICAL PRODUCT

Kim Marienthal, Save A Tree Company

IMPETUS

I was 17 years old when I started the Save A Tree business. The idea came out of the enthusiasm surrounding the first Earth Day on April 22, 1970. At that time I was a high school student working to create a network of environmental groups in the Los Angeles schools. My organization took on the name Attack Contamination Today (ACT). Information dissemination and operation of recycling centers were the main projects.

The literature we distributed suggested ways the individual could reduce pollution, including the suggestion that reusable shopping bags be used in place of paper bags. I did further research on the problems related to manufacture and disposal of paper and plastic bags. I calculated that a single shopper could save one tree per year plus reduce pollution and waste of energy by using a resuable bag. When I discovered there were only a few overpriced shopping bags on the market, I set out to create my own bag.

A friend helped me design a logo incorporating the Save A Tree message. After experimenting with various bags, I located sources for material, printing, and sewing of canvas bags. I acquired a bank loan on the basis of my first purchase orders. I was an environmental activist not yet out of high school finding myself unexpectedly in business.

SUCCESS

My first sales appointment was with a buyer for a major market chain. It took weeks to get in to see him. He gave me 10 minutes at the end of which the gadget on his desk--mechanical chattering teeth--threatened to go off and signal the end of the visit. In the brief time I had, I explained how my bags could improve environmental quality, save the store and customers money, and provide the store with outstanding public relations. He told me, in essence, that ecology and business don't mix. This first failure made me all the more determined to prove ecology and business do mix.

A local market chain in Los Angeles that was promoting environmental products gave me my first order. A number of health food stores, including distributors on the East and West Coasts, followed shortly thereafter. I was well on my way when I entered college.

I entered the University of California at Santa Cruz in 1971. The business ran smoothly, the bags sold themselves, and I was able to devote most of my time to my studies. I decided I wanted to study environmental problems first hand. Through an aggressive field study program at the University, I lined up a summer job with the Environmental Protection Agency (EPA) in Washington, D. C. to work on land use studies. It occurred to me that my work in Washington would me more effective if I did some preparatory studies before leaving California and during my trip across the States. I wrote a study plan which enabled me to get full credit for my studies and endeavored to pay for my travels through sales of my shopping bags.

I learned a great deal about problems of urban planning as well as resource management. I sold bags along the way, especially to college bookstores on campuses where I was interviewing professors. A big surprise came when someone at the Kansas City office of the Federal EPA ordered 2,000 Save A Tree bags--with the EPA logo on the reverse side--for distribution as conference materials and for use as carrying bags for speaking engagements. When I arrived in Washington, D. C. the Director of EPA's Water Programs was sufficiently impressed with the information I had gathered to appoint me as his special assistant on land use problems.

That job was a highlight in my college career and led to two more unique jobs with government agencies. The Save A Tree accounts I picked up during my travels also secured the financing for the rest of my education and further travels. I graduated from Santa Cruz in 1975 with a double major in Economics and Environmental Studies.

I went right into a masters program at the University of California at Berkeley in Environmental Planning. I successfully weaved in a job with the Federal Highway Administration as part of my studies. In my classwork I emphasized energy and transportation and their effect on land use planning. I had every intention of going to work for the Government or a consulting firm upon the completion of my studies. Instead, I pursued Save A Tree bag sales. Since I completed my studies in 1977 my business volume has nearly quadrupled. The cost of paper bags has gone up dramatically, inspiring some market chains --including the first one I went to--to give customers a 3¢ rebate for each reusable bag they bring to the store. One market chain headquartered in Berkeley, California estimated they spent $700,000 on paper bags last year. They are doing a major promotion with Save A Tree bags right now. Indications are that my business will continue to increase.

REFLECTIONS

Today it seems enviornmentalists are always pitted against Business. Business has claimed that environmentalists hamper operations, prevent expansion, and put people out of work. Environmentalists say that Business is destroying the environment without any concern for the future. While there may be some truth to these opposing points of view, I believe this rivalry is unproductive and does nothing to solve environmental and social problems. I hope that my story about Save A Tree clearly demonstrates that it is possible by blending the two to come up with creative solutions to environmental problems.

The overwhelming evidence shows that reusable products, in general, are better for the environment than throwaway products. Reusable products save limited resources, save energy, reduce pollution, litter, and solid waste, and save money over time. **Unfortunately, many big companies seem to operate on misguided** principles that promote throwaway products, produce endless pollution, misuse limited resources, and threaten to degrade the environment beyond its ability to replenish itself. As long as there is a market for environmentally destructive products, compaines will continue to produce such products. So, it is not business, per se, that is to blame, but rather the principle of planned obsolescence carried to the extreme by some big companies. Businesses that are based on the throwaway ethic are leading society on an apocalyptic trend with the slogan "use once, throwaway".

My contention is that, as consumers are made aware of how uneconomical and unecological such products are, they will search out alternatives. At that point, businesses will stop making unecological products. In some cases the Government must step in to provide disincentives to polluting and incentives to stop polluting, but the less regulation, the better. I also believe that as consumers learn how important maintaining an ecological balance is, the free enterprise system provides the mechanism and incentive to fulfill the needs of an enlightened public.

With my training, I have often considered working for the Government or a consulting firm in the environmental field. At one time, I thought this was the only way to bring about social improvement in a healthy environment. For those interested in monitoring pollution control, or researching environmental problems, I wholeheartedly recommend this kind of work. However, I have found that those interested in directly improving the social and physical environment would do better to develop and market environmental products. Environmental activists and researchers are necessary for raising consciousness, but at a certain point action in the form of product development must take place.

Now that I have shown how environmentalists can work with Business, I would suggest that Business stop fighting environmentalists. Existing pollution controls are absolutely necessary for everybody's health--people in business and environmentalists alike. Delays in developing major projects are usually due to poor planning or major design flaws. When the general public has placed a value on a unique resource and wishes to preserve it for posterity, it would be bad business to destroy that resource. As for the myth that environmental legislation costs jobs, it is not true. EPA studies show there has been a net increase in jobs due to environmental mandates. While some people may suffer temporarily as they shift from environmentally destructive jobs to newly created jobs, society as a whole benefits. To build nuclear power plants, produce throwaway products, or make bombs for the sole purpose of creating jobs is dumb. Environmental alternatives are generally labor-intensive. There is too much need for clean energy and better transportation systems and the manufacture of quality products to waste human resources on environmentally destructive products.

In conclusion, Business is not the enemy. On the contrary, I envision a future where many small businesses will provide necessary and environmentally sound products and services. Heavyhanded government regulation will never provide a lasting solution. If we find that solution unacceptable, we should strive for self-sufficient interdependent communities where technology is scaled down to fit our basic needs. Small business responds to environmental needs faster than any government agency ever could. Already, many small businesses are fulfilling a key educational role just by promoting Save A Tree bags. The goal is to measure satisfaction not by the quantity of goods consumed, but rather by the quality of our social and physical environment. I believe that small companies, such as Save A Tree, can help attain that goal.

PART FOUR

THE CONSERVER SOCIETY: HOW DO WE GET THERE?

Focusing on energy and marketing technology, the final part offers one prescription on how to attain the Conserver Society.

A MARKETING APPROACH TO ENERGY CONSERVATION

Arthur Sterngold and Philip Kotler
Northwestern University

INTRODUCTION

Hundreds of laws, regulations and government programs have been adopted to help solve the nation's energy problems. A major part of this effort to fight the "moral equivalent of war" has been programs to encourage people to voluntarily conserve energy. But as President Carter stated in his April 5, 1979, energy policy speech, despite the 1973-74 oil embargo, the revolution in Iran, rapidly rising OPEC oil prices and other symptoms of the energy crisis, "our nation has not yet responded to these warnings." As a result, the President announced the removal of price controls on domestic oil production. Nonetheless, the President continued to emphasize the role of voluntary energy conservation, asking that citizens obey the 55 m.p.h. speed limit and reduce their weekly driving by an average of fifteen miles.

The purpose of this paper is to discuss ways in which marketing concepts can contribute to the cause of voluntary energy conservation. In an age of widespread government intervention in the lives of its citizens, social marketing can be a tool for furthering energy conservation and other social goals in a manner consistent with the principles of a free society. For despite the negative connotations often associated with the term "marketing," it is an approach that attempts to elicit voluntary behavior based on a realistic understanding of people's needs, attitudes and behavior--an orientation often absent from the deliberations of government officials and policy makers.

GOVERNMENT INTERVENTION TO PROMOTE ENERGY DECONSUMPTION

Since the Great Depression of the 1930s, government intervention in the economy and other aspects of life has become more and more pervasive. The ideology of Adam Smith's "invisible hand" has been steadily losing ground to the one of Buckminster Fuller's "spaceship earth." Many people feel that in an age when unbridled technology has the potential to cause widespread destruction (in the form of nuclear war, environmental pollution, etc.) and when the fates of individuals and whole societies are interrelated, major decisions about the future of society should not be left to the free play of market forces, but rather, should be made collectively and consciously through the democratic process. Despite the current popularity of the tax revolt, deregulation and other anti-government movements, today's great debate is not whether society has the right to intervene in the lives of its citizens when facing major social issues, but rather, what forms and vehicles of intervention are most effective and consistent with democratic principles.

The purpose of large-scale government intervention is to produce planned social change--to create social conditions different from those that would have otherwise resulted from the free play of economic, demographic and technological forces. Some forms of planned change are directed at reducing the consumption of goods or services believed to be unhealthy or dangerous, or whose consumption imposes serious costs on the rest of society. Examples are anti-smoking campaigns, the regulation of firearms, nutritional education to decrease the consumption of animal fats, sugar and salt, and programs to encourage water conservation. Of all these interventions, government programs to promote energy conservation probably represent the largest deconsumption effort since the end of the Second World War.

Several approaches have been advocated and employed to promote energy conservation. It is our experience that many government officials and policy makers--particularly those with legal backgrounds--favor <u>legal-regulatory approaches</u>. They argue that the best way to achieve energy deconsumption or other forms of planned social change is through the passage and enforcement of new laws and regulations, using the full weight of the legislative, executive and judicial branches of government. Although current energy problems certainly require some legal-regulatory responses, this approach too often results in unnecessary coercion, conflict, and economic rigidity and inefficiency. And equally important, those who rely on legal-regulatory approaches tend to overlook the needs, attitudes, and situations of the people who have to "live with" and cope with the new laws and regulations. It is the most "heavy-handed" of all the government approaches to planned social change.

Others think in terms of <u>technological approaches</u>, ranging from those who advocate full-scale development of solar energy technologies to others who still believe that nuclear energy will be the panacea to our energy problems. Of course, technological improvements and innovations are important. However, too many people cling to the "promise of technology"--the belief that social problems largely created by modern technology can be solved by even more technology. This view is myopic in two respects. For one, the recent events at Three-Mile Island and growing concern over the dangers of nuclear energy suggest that there are no purely technological solutions to our energy problems. Under any circumstances, the increasing scarcity of conventional energy resources will require major changes in our lifestyles and forms of social organization. At the same time, technology is effective only to the extent that people accept it and use it properly. For example, large numbers of motorists have removed the mandatory anti-pollution equipment from their automobiles to increase mileage and reduce maintenance costs.

Many people argue in favor of economic approaches to solving energy problems--direct or indirect taxes and subsidies to alter the price structure of energy resources, or the use (or removal) of price controls. We agree that economic approaches are critical components of national energy policy. Despite the political consequences, we endorse the President's decision to remove price controls from domestic oil production, so that the prices consumers face at the pump are more informative of the real social costs of gasoline (and we also support the proposal for a windfall profits tax to assist the poor and subsidize the development of alternative energy sources). However, government officials and policy makers sometimes overlook the fact that other variables in addition to price are also important determinants of energy consumption. For example, marketers realize that price often interacts with the other elements of the "marketing mix" in influencing consumption levels. Thus, for example, consumer purchases of home insulation and other energy saving products is not only affected by rapidly rising utility bills, but is also influenced by the availability of these products to consumers, how well-designed and reliable the products are, and the extent to which consumers are aware of these products and how to purchase and use them.

Public information approaches are favored by many people who believe that consumers can be convinced to conserve energy if only given the right information. Again, we agree that information is a key element in any voluntary deconsumption program. However, the process by which people receive, process and act on information has been shown to be highly complex, and influenced by many factors other than the information itself. For example, people will often ignore information--even if actively directed to them as in television or radio commercials-- if they do not already believe that the information will be useful to them. Also, information aimed at changing people's attitudes may be ineffective if it does not lead to behavioral changes and vice versa. Thus, for example, public advertising campaigns aimed at making people more aware of our nation's energy problems are of little value unless that awareness leads to a more energy conserving behavior. At the same time, educating consumers on practical steps they can take to save energy in their homes may be ineffective if the consumers are not already interested in the subject of energy conservation.

Also, as with technology and price, information will interact with other elements of the "marketing mix." Thus government efforts to promote energy conservation through public information campaigns have probably been undermined by government controls that keep the price of oil artificially low, since the information communicated to consumers by price is undoubtedly much more concrete and convincing than public information messages.

Finally, some people advocate community approaches, believing that energy problems can best be solved by people working together in their communities on an inter-personal level. We agree that in order to make energy conservation more familiar, tangible and visible in people's lives--to bring it "closer to home"--local programs, demonstrations and communications are helpful. However, in some cases, those who advocate community approaches overlook the fact that people largely make their energy use decisions as individuals in the marketplace, rather than on a group basis in their communities. For example, in a recent article in Psychology Today, the author noted that the incidence of energy conservation was very high in a community where people actively participated in several community conservation projects. However, this community was located in a very progressive college town, and was specifically designed and promoted to attract people who "were sympathetic to energy conservation, and knew they were signing up to save energy when they bought their houses" (Hamrin 1979, pp. 32-3). Despite the author's conclusion that this study supports Everett Rogers' concepts of diffusion of innovation, there is no evidence to suggest that this community approach could be duplicated on a large scale in more typical American communities.

THE SOCIAL MARKETING APPROACH

The social marketing approach to energy deconsumption is distinguished from these other approaches not because it offers a totally different set of tools and techniques, but because its overall orientation is unique. For our purposes, "social marketing" is defined as an approach to creating planned social change that draws upon concepts and techniques from the marketing field, and attempts to gain people's voluntary cooperation by sensing and satisfying their needs as expressed by their attitudes and behavior. **The social marketing approach** to energy conservation is distinctive in several respects:

1. It is <u>consumer oriented</u> in that the design of energy conservation programs begins with a realistic analysis of consumer needs, attitudes and other characteristics, and if successful, results in consumer satisfaction for having adopted the measures being marketed.

2. It is aimed at eliciting <u>voluntary behavior</u> through the <u>exchange process</u>. It explores ways to encourage consumers to act out of their own self-interest, rather than forcing them to act on the basis of legal or economic sanctions, or expecting them to act out of the same moral sense of duty that motivates the people who are advocating energy conservation.

3. It is <u>holistic</u>, in that the social marketer considers how the several elements of the marketing mix operate separately and together to influence people's adoption of conservation measures.

4. It employs <u>market segmentation</u>, in that different marketing programs (entailing alterations in the marketing mix) are built around different subgroups in the target population, so that the overall effect is greater than if the entire target population had been treated as one homogenous group.

5. It is sensitive to the fact that the <u>consumer adoption process is developmental</u>, and that at different stages in their decision-making process, people are susceptible to different marketing approaches. For example, advertisements stressing the general benefits and need for conservation may be required to make consumers aware and interested in energy conservation. However, for consumers who are already interested and aware, much more specific information on how to evaluate, select and purchase conservation products may be necessary to translate their awareness and interest into actual behavioral responses. [One convenient way of conceptualizing the stages in the adoption process is: (1) awareness, (2) interest, (3) evaluation, (4) adoption, and (5) post-adoption feelings.]

6. It emphasizes the importance of <u>symbolic and subjective meanings</u>, understanding that people make decisions not only on the basis of objective "facts and figures," but that they infer subjective meanings from other

types of information as well (e.g., as when people decide whether or not a smaller, energy-efficient automobile fits their self-image).

7. It is a <u>planned process</u>, in that the marketing program is designed and managed to achieve predetermined results. Although there are many iterations and exceptions to any planning process, one convenient way to conceptualize the major steps in marketing planning is as follows:

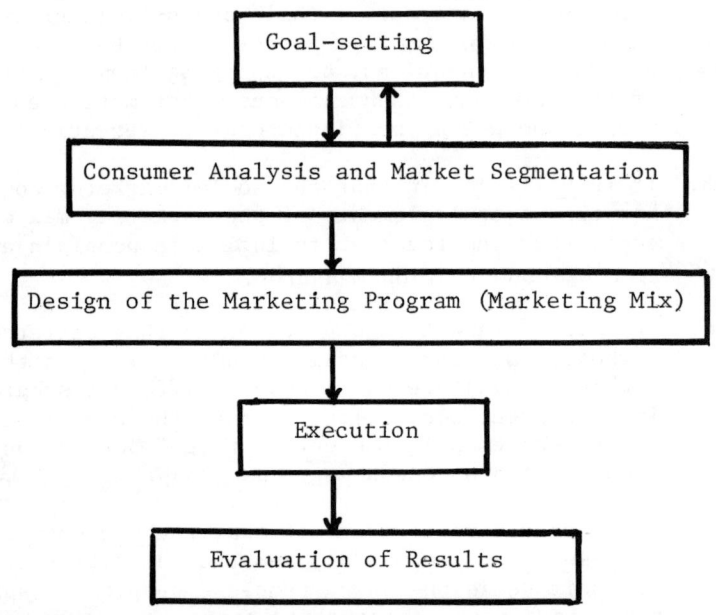

FIGURE 1: MAJOR STAGES IN MARKETING PLANNING

One useful way to describe the variables with which the social marketer has to work (that constitute the marketing mix) are the four P's (McCarthy 1968, pp. 31-33). Business marketers tend to view the problem as one of developing the right <u>product</u> backed by the right <u>promotion</u> and put in the right <u>place</u> at the right <u>price</u>. In the context of social marketing, these four P's can be broadened and a fifth P added: (1) product or program, (2) promotion and publicity, (3) place, (4) price and (5) personal communications.

"Product or program" refers to either the products, services or behavioral changes the social marketer is attempting to get consumers to adopt (e.g., smaller cars, home energy audits, changing the thermostat setting, etc.) or to the design of programs to encourage energy conservation (e.g., workshops, energy fairs, etc.). "Price" refers to all important financial or nonmonetary costs people face in adopting these products, services or behavioral changes, or in participating in programs. Often, nonmonetary costs such as time, inconvenience and "hassle" are a greater burden to people than monetary costs. "Place" refers to the distribution channels and outlets through which products and programs are made available (e.g., home insulation is sold at lumber yards and hardware stores, workshops are often given at schools and community centers, etc.) "Promotion and publicity" refer to all forms of communication other than inter-personal forms (e.g., advertising, newspaper articles, posters, etc.). Finally, personal communication refers to all inter-personal forms of contact (e.g., telephone calls, meetings, door-to-door solicitation, personal selling, etc.).

The five P's are a somewhat arbitrary and simplistic method of describing the marketing mix, and in some cases are ambiguous. Nonetheless, they illustrate social marketing's holistic approach to accomplishing social objectives. Of the five alternative approaches to energy conservation discussed earlier, four can be seen as related to one of the "five P's" of social marketing: technological approaches have to do with "product" design, economic approaches with "price," public information approaches with "promotion and publicity," and community approaches fall under "personal communications." Thus, with the exception of legal-regulatory approaches, social marketing may be viewed as overlapping with the other approaches to planned social change.

CONSUMER ANALYSIS

Numerous studies have been done on people's attitudes and behavior regarding energy issues. Rather than review these past studies, we will summarize some of the key findings from consumer research conducted by one of the authors in conjunction with the Evanston Environmental Association of Evanston, Illinois. This project involved open-ended intervews with over twenty individuals during the 1978-79 winter, most of whom were homeowners. (The remaining sections of this paper are restricted to a discussion of energy conservation in people's residences). Although we certainly do not suggest that the findings from these interviews are representative of the general population, we do feel they offer some fresh insights into the problems of energy conservation.

Most of the respondents said they had considered adopting some energy conservation measures during the previous year, but few had actually done so. When it came to behavioral actions such as turning down thermostats or driving less, most people said comfort and convenience were the major reasons for not conserving energy. On the other hand, when considering more substantial conservation measures, such as adding insulation to their homes or purchasing a new water heater, many people said that cost was the main obstacle. However, many of these same people were aware that such conservation measures would save them money in the long run, and in addition, many of these respondents were financially well off.

For these reasons, we decided to probe more deeply into why people resisted purchasing and installing energy conserving products. For one, we found that many people simply did not want to devote the necessary time and effort to investigate, evaluate and select the right products for their homes. As one man said, "I probably could save some money by putting in storm windows, but right now I just don't want to bother with it." Another person said he had considered replacing the insulation under his roof, but had not pursued this because "my attic is loaded with junk--we'd probably have to spend a whole day just cleaning it before they could even get to the insulation." To most people, thinking about and adopting energy conserving products, services or behaviors is not a familiar or routine task, and to many people the time, effort and "bother" seem to be significant nonmonetary costs.

Another major barrier some respondents faced in considering conservation actions was their lack of confidence and knowledge in dealing with what they considered to be "technical matters." This factor seemed to have several dimensions. Some people mentioned a fear of "being taken" by unscrupulous contractors or merchants, since they lacked the basic knowledge to select and evaluate the right products. Others felt incompetent in dealing with the entire issue of conservation, believing it to be too complicated or technical for them to understand. As one elderly man stated, "I keep asking my sons to come over and help--I wouldn't know where to start."

Other people commented that although they had considered adopting conservation measures, they had not proceeded because they were not sure "what to do next." Some respondents mentioned that although they were aware of conservation issues, it was not something relevant or visible in their lives. One homeowner stated, "If saving energy was so important, I'd hear more about it. No one around here seems terribly concerned about it."

Finally, several people were skeptical that they could save as much money on energy conserving measures as had been suggested to them by free energy audits they had received from the government (Project Conserve), or they were uncertain about the reliability and performance of conservation products.

Of the people who had adopted some energy conservation measures in the recent past, increasing the comfort level in the home was mentioned as frequently as saving money as the main motivation. This was true mostly among people who mentioned that they had installed additional insulation in their homes, purchased storm windows and doors, or weatherized their homes. This is understandable in light of the extremely cold winters during the last two years.

Some tentative conclusions may be drawn from these findings. For one, it seems that people's attitudes and behavior regarding energy conservation are significantly influenced by factors other than money--comfort, convenience, time, effort, "bother," etc. These nonmonetary factors should be considered in efforts to market conservation.

In addition, many people may feel incompetent in dealing with what they believe to be "technical matters" associated with energy conservation, which can lead to apprehensions over "being taken" by unscrupulous merchants or contractors, not knowing how to follow up on one's interest in conservation measures, or feeling that one will have to invest a great deal of personal time and effort in order to conserve energy. Social marketing programs should address these obstacles to conservation behavior.

Finally, many people may feel that energy conservation is a distant issue, and that it is not something that is relevant and conspicuous in their lives and communities. A goal of social marketing should be to bring energy conservation "closer to home," which may require more localized programs in people's communities, with more emphasis on personal communications.

MARKET SEGMENTATION

As previously discussed, the idea of market segmentation is that different marketing approaches (involving alterations in the marketing mix) are used to reach different subgroups in the population. Usually, some degree of segmentation will produce better results than treating all consumers as one mass market. At the same time, there is a point beyond which too much segmentation becomes impractical or inefficient. How many and which subgroups to treat as separate market segments is a matter of managerial judgment.

When it comes to marketing energy conservation to the residential sector, homeowners and renters may require different marketing approaches. Homeowners are freer to make structural improvements in their homes (e.g., adding insulation or a new water heater), and because they own their homes and tend to live in them for a longer period of time than do renters, they have more to gain from conservation measures that require larger initial outlays. Thus, homeowners are probably a better market for substantial conservation actions involving structural changes in the home, whereas renters may be a more appropriate target for stressing behavioral actions, such as adjusting their thermostats, etc. In addition, communications aimed at renters could provide them with arguments to persuade their landlords to make structural improvements in their buildings.

Size and type of residential structure may be another basis for segmenting the market. For one, because they are larger and generally have more of their surface area exposed to the outside, the potential for conserving energy per single-family dwelling is greater than per apartment in multi-family dwellings. Also, since the incidence of home ownership is highest among single-family homes, their residents may be most interested in costly structural improvements that will save the greatest amount of energy. For these reasons, single-family dwellings may be a higher priority for conservation programs whose primary goal is simply to reduce overall levels of energy consumption.

The benefits people seek in considering conservation measures may also be a basis for segmenting the market. The three major reasons for conservation seem to be to save money, to increase the comfort of the home, and to help the nation solve its energy problems. All three benefits should be stressed in mass communications, and in more selective communications, those benefits should be stressed that are most appropriate to the target audiences.

People who are moving into new homes may be a prime market segment for conservation programs. For one, new residents are often accessible through marketing intermediaries--lending institutions, realtors, moving companies and home builders. These intermediaries could possibly be used as channels through which to deliver conservation messages and materials, such as "how to" conservation workbooks. Also, it is often at this stage that people make structural improvements in their homes and settle into new living patterns. Consequently, they may be particularly responsive to suggesitons on how to save energy.

Many other subgroups are candidates for market segments to be approached by different marketing programs, including students, senior citizens, people who are active in social and community organizations, individuals who enjoy working on their homes and "do-it-yourself" projects, consumers who already have favorable attitudes toward energy conservation, families in different income classes and locations, etc. As always, the decision to identify and select different market segments for special marketing approaches is based on judgment as to what will be most practical and effective.

RECOMMENDATIONS

Based on the consumer interviews mentioned above, on other studies of people's attitudes and behavior regarding energy issues, and on the authors' own ideas, this section offers a potpourri of recommendations for marketing energy conservation to residences. The proposals are categorized according to the "five P's" defined earlier.

Product and Program Design

1. Retailers, contractors and other firms with an interest in selling energy conservation products and services should be encouraged to offer conservation "systems" or "packages" that are designed to meet consumer needs in one convenient process, rather than requiring consumers to piece together several products and services, or to undergo several steps in adopting conservation measures.

2. Based on a "foot-in-the-door" strategy, local governments should consider organizing groups of knowledgeable employees or volunteers to offer free home energy audits to local residents. These audits should be conducted with household members as active participants in the audit process, so that there can be a great deal of personal communication between auditors and residents. At the same time, the auditors

can help answer questions about how to follow up on the recommendations. Local merchants who sell energy conserving products and services may be willing to help subsidize this program.

Place

3. Energy conservation "hotlines" should be established at the local level, staffed by knowledgeable volunteers or government employees, to serve as "response channels" through which consumers can get answers to specific questions.

Price

4. Commercial banks, S&L's and other lending institutions should be encouraged to make loans available to people to finance energy conserving projects in their homes, and to consider the energy costs of home ownership when evaluating mortgage applications.

Promotion and Publicity

5. Energy conservation advertisements aimed at mass markets should stress three benefits of conservation actions: saving money, increasing the comfort of the home, and helping the nation solve its energy problems.

6. Promotion and publicity aimed at encouraging conservation behavior, rather than only increasing energy awareness, should tell people what specific actions are recommended, how they will benefit from those actions, and how to get further information (e.g., "In a typical home in Evanston, installing storm windows and doors can save you up to 20% on your heating and air conditioning bills, and at the same time, will make your home more comfortable by eliminating annoying cold and hot spots. Storm windows and doors are available at most hardware stores and lumber yards in the Evanston area. For further information, contact the Evanston Energy Hotline by calling ...").

7. Energy conservation messages should be made more personal and relevant to consumers by incorporating "real life" examples and testimonials with which

consumers can personally relate (e.g., "Local resident John Doe could care less about saving energy until he discovered that he could save $100 per year on his utility bills by replacing the insulation in his walls and ceiling. Chances are that damaged or inadequate insulation in your home is costing you money, too").

8. To help compensate for the fact that many people are skeptical about the cost-savings from conservation actions, as much tangible evidence as possible should be provided on how conservation behavior can save money (e.g., showing photographs of before-and-after utility bills, testimonials, etc.).

9. "Do-it-yourself" workbooks should be developed and widely distributed that contain a hierarchy of home conservation programs that differ in complexity, cost and completeness, so that consumers can find the program that best matches their level of interest, expertise and financial resources. Local stores that sell conservation products and services could assist in financing and distributing the workbooks.

Personal Communications

10. Local communities should sponsor energy conservation fairs, workshops and other events that allow for "audience participation" and "hands on" experiences in which consumers can actively participate in some forms of simulated or real conservation behavior. In general, these events should be structured to give people a tangible "feel" for conservation behavior and to provide them with successful task experiences to help overcome feelings of incompetence (as is done in many cooking and craft courses).

11. Local government should be encouraged to build highly visible and well-publicized conservation demonstration projects, such as at fire stations, schools, libraries and other public buildings. In addition to actually helping conserve energy in these facilities, the projects would also serve as tangible evidence of local government's commitment to energy conservation.

12. Special conservation programs should be designed for young people through schools, churches and synagogues,

youth organizations, etc. In addition to teaching them about energy conservation, the students should be encouraged to help "spread the word" and provide basic information on how to conserve energy to other family members and neighbors.

CONCLUSIONS

The purpose of this paper has been to discuss how the marketing way of thinking can contribute to the cause of energy conservation. We emphasized the point that marketing is a valuable approach not because it offers a totally new set of tools and techniques, but rather, because its overall orientation to creating social change is different from those approaches most commonly employed in the public sector. The most important feature of the social marketing approach is that it aims at eliciting voluntary behavior based on the self-interest of consumers by paying close attention to their needs, attitudes and other characteristics.

The psychologist Rollo May has pointed out that the conscious theories of psychologists often become the unconscious impulses of patients. An analogous situation often occurs in government, where policies and programs are often more heavily based on the professional biases, political ideologies or bureaucratic interests of public officials than on a realistic understanding of the needs of the people who have to "live with" those policies and programs. This may be one reason why government is so widely perceived as overly bureaucratic and unresponsive to the needs of citizens[1].

In an era of widespread government intervention in people's lives, a social marketing orientation can provide a healthy balance to these more elitist approaches to creating social change.

---

[1] A similar point was made by Mary Gardiner Jones in a speech she gave just prior to the conclusion of her term as an FTC commissioner. In that speech, she spoke favorably of what she perceived to be a change in the FTC's basic orientation: "The essential shift in the Commission's performance has been in its recognition and concern for the problems confronting the individual citizen as he confronts the market place rather than its previous much more legalistic view of its role," in Laurence P. Feldman (1976), Consumer Protection: Problems and Prospects, New York, N.Y.: West Publishing Co., p. 264.

REFERENCES

Hamrin, Jan (1979), "Energy-Saving Homes: Don't Bet on Technology Alone," <u>Psychology Today</u>, Vol. 12, No. 11 (April).

McCarthy, E. Jerome (1968), <u>Basic Marketing: A Managerial Approach</u>, 3rd edition, Homewood, IL: Richard D. Irwin, Inc.